BEST OF

Paris

Terry Carter

Best of Paris
3rd edition – July 2005
First published – April 2000

Published by Lonely Planet Publications Pty Ltd
ABN 36 005 607 983

Australia	Head Office, Locked Bag 1, Footscray, Vic 3011
	☎ 03 8379 8000 fax 03 8379 8111
	🖳 talk2us@lonelyplanet.com.au
USA	150 Linden St, Oakland, CA 94607
	☎ 510 893 8555 toll free 800 275 8555
	fax 510 893 8572
	🖳 info@lonelyplanet.com
UK	72–82 Rosebery Avenue, London EC1R 4RW
	☎ 020 7841 9000 fax 020 7841 9001
	🖳 go@lonelyplanet.co.uk

This title was commissioned in Lonely Planet's London office and produced by: **Commissioning Editor** Sam Trafford **Coordinating Editor** Melissa Faulkner **Coordinating Cartographer** Simon Tillema **Layout Designer** John Shippick **Editor** Nancy Ianni **Indexer** Melissa Faulkner **Managing Cartographer** Mark Griffiths **Cover Designer** Julie Rovis **Project Managers** Charles Rawlings-Way and Rachel Imeson **Mapping Development** Paul Piaia **Thanks to** Martin Heng and Sally Darmody

© Lonely Planet Publications Pty Ltd 2005.

Photographs by Lonely Planet Images, Jean-Bernard Carillet & Jonathan Smith except for the following: p38 Olivier Cirendini/Lonely Planet Images, p80 Greg Elms/Lonely Planet Images, p40, p86, p105 Rob Flynn/Lonely Planet Images, p46 John Hay/Lonely Planet Images, p14, p30 Martin Moos/Lonely Planet Images, p20 Adina Tovy Amsel/Lonely Planet Images, p20 Brent Winebrenner/Lonely Planet Images. **Cover photograph** Pont Alexandre III and canal tour boat, Chris Cheadle/Getty Images. All images are copyright of the photographers unless otherwise indicated. Many of the images in this guide are available for licensing from Lonely Planet Images: 🖳 www.lonelyplanetimages.com

ISBN 1740594797

Printed by Markono Print Media Pte Ltd, Singapore

Acknowledgements Many thanks to the RATP for the use of its transit map © RATP – CML Agence Cartographique

HOW TO USE THIS BOOK

Colour-Coding & Maps

Each chapter has a colour code along the banner at the top of the page which is also used for text and symbols on maps (eg all venues reviewed in the Highlights chapter are orange on the maps). The fold-out maps inside the front and back covers are numbered from 1 to 5. All sights and venues in the text have map references; eg, (4, B3) means Map 4, grid reference B3. See p128 for map symbols.

Prices

Multiple prices listed with reviews (eg €10/5) usually indicate adult/concession admission to a venue. Concession prices can include senior, student, member or coupon discounts. Meal cost and room rate categories are listed at the start of the Eating and Sleeping chapters, respectively.

Text Symbols

- ☎ telephone
- ✉ address
- 🖳 email/website address
- $ admission
- ☷ opening hours
- ⓘ information
- Ⓜ metro
- 🚍 bus
- Ⓟ parking available
- ♿ wheelchair access
- ✗ on site/nearby eatery
- 🚼 child-friendly venue
- Ⓥ good vegetarian selection

Contents

From the Publisher

AUTHOR

Terry Carter

The first taste of Paris came from Terry's high-school French teacher on Bastille Day. His *bresse bleu* cheese offering to students was rejected by all but Terry. His teacher declared that, although Terry's French-language skills left a lot to be desired, his eating skills passed the grade.

Terry worked in the travel publishing industry in Australia before the photographic slides of travel destinations became too much. Now living in Dubai, he spends a couple of months each year exploring European cities, especially places known for their food and wine. Terry has a Master's degree in media studies and does freelance travel writing, photography and Web design.

Thanks foremost to my wife and lifelong travelling partner, Lara Dunston, for her help with shopping in Paris and for putting up with me during the write-up. Many thanks to Sandrine Rastello for her help and to the various people who offered advice during my stay in Paris.

The 1st and 2nd editions of this book were written by Rob Flynn.

PHOTOGRAPHER

Jean-Bernard Carillet

A Paris-based author and photographer, Jean-Bernard's photos have appeared in many Lonely Planet guides, including *Best of Brussels* and *Naples & the Amalfi Coast*. When not in the tropics or markets in Eastern Africa, he heads for eastern France, southern Belgium and the Ruhr in Germany to capture the industrial wasteland. He was all too happy to photograph from his doorstep and rediscover his city. As a true-blue Parisian, he confirms that Paris is the City of Light.

Jonathan Smith

Raised in the Scottish Highlands, Jonathan completed a Master's degree in German from the University of St Andrews. After trying language teaching and translating Lithuanian cookery books, Jon became a freelance travel photographer. Jon was in his element exploring Parisian café society, in the footsteps of his photographic idol Henri Cartier-Bresson.

SEND US YOUR FEEDBACK

We love to hear from travellers – your comments keep us on our toes and help make our books better. Our well-travelled team reads every word on what you loved or loathed about this book. Although we cannot reply individually to postal submissions, we always guarantee that your feedback goes straight to the appropriate authors, in time for the next edition – and the most useful submissions are rewarded with a free book. To send us your updates – and find out about Lonely Planet events, newsletters and travel news – visit our award-winning website: 🖥 **www.lonelyplanet.com/feedback.**

Note: We may edit, reproduce and incorporate your comments in Lonely Planet products such as guidebooks, websites and digital products, so let us know if you don't want your comments reproduced or your name acknowledged. For a copy of our privacy policy visit 🖥 www.lonelyplanet.com/privacy.

Introducing Paris

Who the hell does Paris think it is? All that art, culture, history and romance. Yet this city remains so aloof. You don't want to fall for someone who doesn't care. So you try to act cool. The Eiffel Tower? It's not that big. The Louvre? It's too big. The hotel room? Too cramped. The streets? Too busy. That intimate *prix fixe* (set-priced *menu*) restaurant that you found where you had a small vineyard champagne and a dozen oysters that burst with the flavours of Brittany? You're in love.

To many travellers, Paris is a checklist of iconic buildings and old art. Sure, do the sights; they are sublime. Visit the museums; they are the best in the world. But Paris is more than just eye candy – it's total sensory overload. Indulge in the sounds of opera, jazz or catch some world music acts that reflect Paris' multicultural mix. It's olfactory heaven; visit a perfume boutique and enjoy the fragrance of fresh buttery croissants. It's a city to feel; touch the fabric of a stunning couture gown, or experience that tingling *frisson* of fear and pleasure when you take your first peek from atop the Tour Eiffel. It's a city to savour; with impeccable *haute cuisine,* fresh seafood and rich chocolates.

The best part is, Paris now seems to care that you're having a good time. The hotels are better, the restaurants are more diverse and the Parisians more welcoming. The world's most romantic city is now more seductive than ever.

Even the Métropolitain is cosmopolitan

Neighbourhoods

Paris has 20 *arrondissements,* spiralling clockwise from its centre to the Périphérique (ring road). The last two numbers of a postcode define the *arrondissement* and these are noted throughout the book. Paris' has distinctive *quartiers* (quarters), which overlap several *arrondissements.*

The Seine's two islands, **Île de la Cité** (1er, and home to Notre Dame, p9) and **Île St-Louis** (4e, p15), are at Paris' centre. **Louvre** and **Les Halles** (1er, part of 2e and 4e) are host to the **Musée du Louvre** (p11) as well as **Centre Pompidou** (p13). Next door are the atmospheric **Marais** (3e and 4e, p17) and gentrified **Bastille** district (11e).

The Left Bank is where to find the **Latin Quarter**, the original centre of learning, and to its southeast the leafy **Jardin des Plantes** (both 5e). To the southwest of here are the shops, galleries and cafés of chic **St-Germain** and **Odéon** (both 6e). To the north of these are **Faubourg St-Germain** and **Invalides** (both 7e, p18) plus the **Eiffel Tower** (p8).

Across the Seine is the genteel 16e with its grand apartments and broad streets. To the east of here are the **Arc de Triomphe** and **av des Champs-Élysées** (both 8e, p10), leading eastward to **La Défense** p26, which ends at **Concorde**, and

> ### Off the Beaten Track
> A peaceful spot in the city's heart is **place Dauphine** (5, B2; Ⓜ Pont Neuf), tucked near Île de la Cité's western end. Smart redevelopment ideas have seen former elevated railway **Promenade Plantée** (2, G4; Ⓜ Bastille, Reuilly Diderot) become a serene walkway, while **Parc de Bercy** (2, H5; Ⓜ Bercy) with its redeveloped wine warehouses benefits from the neighbouring Seine. To really escape the hubbub head to the **Bois de Boulogne** (2, A4; Ⓜ Porte Dauphine, Porte Maillot, Porte d'Auteuil) in the 16e or the **Bois de Vincennes** (2, J5; Ⓜ Château de Vincennes) in the 12e.

to the north of that is **Madeleine**; both are historic *places* or squares. To their southeast are the city's original **Opéra** area and there are the **Grands Boulevards** (both 9e) lined with massive department stores.

Revolutionised place de la Bastille

The 10e has busy city rail hubs, **Gare du Nord** and **Gare de l'Est**, plus hip **Canal St-Martin**. To the city's east (in 20e) is the working-class **Belleville** and to the south is **Ménilmontant**, with edgy bars.

To the south is the revamped area of **Bercy**. Across the Seine is the 13e, home of the grandiose national library and **Chinatown**.

To the north is **Montmartre** (p16, 18e) and **Pigalle**, the tame red-light district. **La Villette** (19e) has cool museums butted against the city's northeast edge.

Itineraries

DAY ONE

Book dinner first (p71). Join a half-day **tour** (p48) or embark on a **cruise** (p47) along the Seine. Then concentrate on the Parisian icons: **Cathédrale du Notre Dame** (p9), the **Musée du Louvre** (p11), the **Arc de Triomphe** (p10) and the **Eiffel Tower** (p8) in the late afternoon. Head to **av des Champs-Élysées** (p10) for some shopping and then on to dinner.

DAY TWO

Art lovers should head straight for the **Musée d'Orsay** (p12) or the **Centre Pompidou** (p13). Alternatively **Ste-Chapelle** (p14), **Musée National du Moyen Âge** (p22) or the **Musée Rodin** (p23), or all three, are worthwhile choices. Check out the village atmosphere of **Montmartre** (p16) in the afternoon, dinner in the **Marais** (p17) followed by a neighbourhood stroll or drinks in one of the great bars.

Lowlights
- Attempting to take in the sights while dodging doggy-doo.
- Trying to have quality time with Mona Lisa amid the digital cameras.
- Hotel rooms might be getting better, but they're sure not getting bigger.
- Finding a great restaurant, but not understanding one word of *la carte (from the menu)*.

DAY THREE

With another day up your sleeve, walk through the **Cimetière du Père Lachaise** (p19), or **Parc de la Villette** (p25) and perhaps spend time in the **Jardin du Luxembourg** (p21). Take in a concert, opera or ballet at the **Palais Garnier** (p33) or **Opéra Bastille** (p33), followed by a bistro dinner and bar-hopping (p83).

ONE WEEK

If you have one week, visit places 'outside the walls' such as **La Défense** (p26) and **St-Denis** (p34), and take a day trip to **Château de Versailles** (p20) or **Château de Fontainebleau** (p45).

JEAN-BERNARD CARILLET

Feeling high and mighty from Montmartre's Sacre Cœur overlooking Paris

Highlights

EIFFEL TOWER (3, A4)

It's hard to believe that when Gustave Eiffel's iconic tower was under construction for the 1889 Exposition Universelle (World Fair), it was criticised as a 'Tower of Babel', 'useless and monstrous'. The critics were silenced when two million visitors ascended the tower in the first year and to date 210 million visitors have made the pilgrimage. Eiffel was indignant that critics assumed that his engineering brilliance didn't extend to a love of aesthetics. The elegance and economy of his design has assured the tower's place in architectural history.

INFORMATION

- ☎ 01 44 11 23 23
- 🖥 www.tour-eiffel.fr
- ✉ Champ de Mars, 7e
- € lift €4-10.40; stairway €3.50
- 🕐 lifts 9.30am-11pm Sep–mid-Jun, 9am-midnight mid-Jun–Aug; stairs 9.30am-6.30pm Sep–mid-Jun, 9am-midnight mid-Jun–Aug
- ⓘ guided tours (can be in English; book ahead) ☎ 01 44 54 19 30
- Ⓜ Bir Hakeim
- ♿ 1st & 2nd fl
- ✗ café & Altitude 95 bar/restaurant, Jules Verne restaurant (p80)

JONATHAN SMITH

DON'T MISS

- Views at dusk and the light show (on the hour, 10min)
- Gustave Eiffel's 3rd fl office
- The ice-skating rink on the first level in winter

JEAN-BERNARD CARILLET

The ultimate Iron Maiden

The tower is 320m high, which can vary as much as 15cm, since the 7000-tonne iron tower (bolted with 2.5 million rivets) expands in warm weather and contracts when it's cold. It was the world's tallest structure until Manhattan's Chrysler Building was finished in 1930. Enjoying the **panoramic views** from any of the three levels (57m, 115m and 276m) is breathtaking. If you're lucky enough to ascend on a perfect day, the view from the top extends 60km. If you're fit, you can avoid the lift queues by walking up the stairs in the south pillar to the 1st or 2nd platforms.

CATHÉDRALE DE NOTRE DAME DE PARIS (5, C3)

This Gothic masterpiece, Cathedral of Our Lady of Paris, on the **Île de la Cité** (p15), is the metaphorical and literal heart of Paris. Built on a site first occupied by a Roman temple and then two earlier Christian churches, the first stone was laid by Pope Alexander III in 1163

INFORMATION

- ☎ 01 42 34 56 10
- 🖳 www.monum.fr
- ✉ place du Parvis, 4e
- € tower/crypt €5.35/3.80
- ⏱ cathedral 8am-7pm (closed 12.30-2pm Sat); towers 9.30am-7.30pm Apr-Sep, 10am-5pm Oct-Mar
- ℹ 1hr guided tours (in English) noon Wed-Thu & 2.30pm Sat (daily Aug)
- Ⓜ Cité
- ♿ access to cathedral
- ✕ Brasserie de l'Île St-Louis (p77)

DON'T MISS

- 14th-century chancel screen
- Viollet-le-Duc's 19th-century central spire
- Portal to the Virgin
- Charles Le Brun's 'May' paintings

and it was finally completed about 1330. Distances to every part of metropolitan France are measured from **point zéro**, a bronze star in **place du Parvis Notre Dame**.

The cathedral's immense interior is a feat of medieval engineering and can accommodate over 6000 worshippers. Exceptional features include the **7800-pipe organ** and the spectacular **rose windows**, the 10m window over the west façade has remained virtually unchanged since the 13th century.

Climbing the 387 steps of the **north tower** brings you to the top of the **west façade**, where you and the **gargoyles** witness a spectacular view of Paris. The best view of the **flying buttresses** – a Gothic technical innovation used to support the sheer walls and roof of the chancel – is from **Square Jean XXIII**, the appealing park behind the cathedral.

Mind your manners (the saints are watching)

JEAN-BERNARD CARILLET

ARC DE TRIOMPHE & CHAMPS ÉLYSÉES (3, B1)

After Napoleon's stunning victory at Austerlitz in 1805, the multitasking 'little corporal' commissioned a triumphal arch in 1806. The Arc towers 50m above place Charles de Gaulle or place d'Étoile (Star Place), so named because of the 12 grand boulevards that radiate from there. The most famous of the four high-relief panels on the Arc is François Rude's **Départ des Volontaires de 1792** (Departure of the Volunteers of 1792), also called *La Marseillaise* (France's national anthem).

INFORMATION

- ☎ 01 55 37 73 77
- 🖳 www.monum.fr
- ✉ place Charles de Gaulle, 8e
- € viewing platform €8/5
- 🕑 10am-10.30pm Oct-Mar; to 11pm Apr-Sep
- ℹ guided tours (in French) €7/4.50
- Ⓜ Charles de Gaulle-Étoile
- ♿ limited

JEAN-BERNARD CARILLET

From the top of the Arc (284 steps) you can look straight down the av des Champs Élysées, to the place de la Concorde. Today the Arc is a potent symbol of French national spirit, but its instigator never lived to see it finished. It was completed in 1836, which was 15 years after Napoleon's death.

The grandest boulevard running off the Arc de Triomphe is the 2km-long av des Champs Élysées, popular with the aristocracy of the mid-19th century who frequented its cafés and theatres. Today, while the avenue finds itself hamstrung by traffic, ho-hum retail outlets and car showrooms, there are some signs that it's regaining the spark of its glory years.

Triumphant March

Among the armies to march triumphantly through the arch and down the av des Champs Élysées were the Germans in 1871, the Allies in 1919, the Germans again in 1940 and the Allies once more in 1944.

JONATHAN SMITH

Lest we forget Napolean's triumphs

MUSÉE DU LOUVRE (5, B1)

Perhaps the world's greatest art museum, to many visitors the sheer size of this former fortress makes it just as daunting to conquer. The fruits of human civilisation, from antiquity to the 19th century are on offer, so the meticulous planning of a military campaign is necessary to get the most from your visit.

The massive Palais du Louvre was created by Philippe-Auguste in the early 13th century and rebuilt in the mid-16th century. The Revolutionary Convention converted it into a national museum in 1793. The 'Grand Louvre' project (totalling €1.07 billion), was inaugurated by the late President François Mitterrand in 1989, doubling the museum's exhibition space, and included the once controversial Pyramid that's now a permanent fixture of Louvre postcards.

INFORMATION
- ☎ 01 40 20 53 17
- 🖳 www.louvre.fr
- ✉ Palais du Louvre, place du Louvre 1er
- € €7.50/5 (€5 Sun); free 1st Sun of month
- ⊙ 9am-9.45pm Mon & Wed, to 6pm Thu-Sun
- ⓘ 1½hr-guided tours (in English) 11am, 2pm & 3pm Mon-Sat €6/3.50
- Ⓜ Palais-Royal Musée du Louvre
- ♿ OK
- ✗ food court, restaurants, cafés

DON'T MISS
- IM Pei's glass pyramid
- Cour Carrée by night
- Richelieu Wing sculpture gardens
- Sackler Wing of Oriental Antiquities

Mannerism versus postmodernism

JEAN-BERNARD CARILLET

In view of the museum's sheer scale, pick up one of the useful map-guides and highlight the works you're aching to see. The **antiquities** – Oriental, Egyptian, Greek and Roman – are dazzling, the European painting collection (1400–1848) is comprehensive and the *objets d'art* are very eclectic, but unless you have days to spare you will be making some tough decisions.

Visiting this immense gallery's signature painting, Leonardo da Vinci's *La Jaconde*, or **Mona Lisa**, is still essential. While the world's most well-known half-smile is a wonderful example of da Vinci's brilliance, the bulletproof glass case and flashing cameras that surround her make for less than optimal viewing.

MUSÉE D'ORSAY (3, E3)

This former railway station houses a spectacular variety of French **Art Nouveau**, **impressionist** and **postimpressionist** works, making it a definite stop for any art lover. Chronologically sandwiched between the works of the Louvre (p11) and the Centre Pompidou (opposite), the museum shows France's national collection of paintings, sculptures and *objets d'art* from 1848 to 1914. Designed by Victor Laloux and built for the 1900 Exposition Universelle, the station was earmarked for demolition until the late '70s, when it was agreed to make it into a museum.

While the museum is designed in chronological order from the ground floor up, most visitors head for the skylight-illuminated upper floor (1870–1914), where the famous impressionist paintings by Monet, Renoir, Pissarro, Sisley, Dégas and Manet and the

INFORMATION
- ☎ 01 40 49 48 14
- 🖳 www.musee -orsay.fr
- ✉ 1 rue de la Légion d'Honneur, 7e
- € €7/5
- ⏲ 9am-6pm Tue, Wed, Fri & Sat, to 9.45pm Thu, 9am-6pm Sun late Jun–Sep, 10am-6pm Tue, Wed, Fri & Sat, to 9.45pm Thu, 9am-6pm Sun Oct-Jun
- ⓘ guided tours (in English) Tue-Sat 11.30am, Thu 4pm Feb-Aug €6/4.50; 1½hr
- Ⓜ Solférino
- ♿ good
- 🍴 café

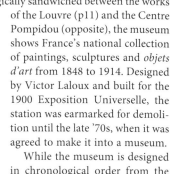

postimpressionist works of Van Gogh, Cézanne, Seurat and Matisse reside. Away from the consistent crowds, the ground floor (1848–70) has an eclectic sculpture gallery; François Rude's *Spirit of the Fatherland* is a fragment of his famous **La Marseillaise** relief for the Arc de Triomphe, while Jean-Baptiste Carpeaux's exuberant *The Dance* scandalised Paris in 1868. Smaller galleries feature key works from the classical and realist movements, including Ingres' *The Source* and Millet's *The Gleaners,* and Manet's provocative **Olympia** and *Lunch in the Grass.*

DON'T MISS
- Van Gogh's *Room at Arles* and Renoir's *Dancing at Le Moulin de la Galette*
- Rodin sculptures *(Balzac* and *Gates of Hell)* and the Art Nouveau collection
- The former station's enormous clock

A *dégustation* menu for impressionist art

CENTRE POMPIDOU (5, D1)

Inaugurated in 1977, the Centre National d'Art et de Culture Georges Pompidou (Georges Pompidou National Centre of Art & Culture) has

been a stunning success, praised for its outstanding collection of modern art and the building that accommodates it. To maximise exhibition space, the architects Renzo Piano and Richard Rogers put the building's 'insides' on the outside. While an important architectural exercise, time hasn't eased the building's contextual insensitivity with its surrounds.

The open space at ground level, **Forum du Centre Pompidou**, houses temporary exhibits. The 4th and 5th floors of the centre exhibit a fraction of the 50,000-plus works of the **Musée National d'Art Moderne** (MNAM), France's extensive national collection of art dating from 1905 onwards, including important works of the Surrealists and Cubists, as well as pop art and contemporary pieces.

The **Bibliothèque Publique d'Information** (BPI) is huge, and takes up the 1st (a section), 2nd and 3rd floors. The 6th floor has more temporary exhibition space and Georges restaurant (p69) with panoramic views. There are cinemas and other entertainment venues on the 1st floor and in the basement.

INFORMATION
- ☎ 01 44 78 12 33
- 🖥 www.centrepompidou.fr
- ✉ place Georges Pompidou, 4e
- € day passes €10/8, MNAM €7/5, under 13s free
- 🕙 forum 11am-10pm Wed-Mon; MNAM to 9pm Wed-Mon; BPI noon-10pm Mon & Wed-Fri, 11am-10pm Sat & Sun
- ⓘ information desks on 1st fl
- Ⓜ Rambuteau
- ♿ good, access through Atelier Brancusi
- ✗ Georges (p69)

At least the paintings are on the inside

Place Georges Pompidou, west of the Centre, attracts countless buskers, while on adjacent place Igor Stravinsky, the **mechanical fountains** of skeletons, dragons and other fanciful creations are a kids' favourite.

DON'T MISS
- Exterior colour-coding of the building's functions
- Views from the roof terrace
- Works by Georges Braque, Marc Chagall, Henri Matisse, Pablo Picasso and Suzanne Valadon

STE-CHAPELLE (5, C2)

This Gothic gem, tucked away within the walls of the **Palais de Justice** (Law Courts), is masterpiece of delicacy and finesse. The 'walls' of the upper chapel (built for worship by the king and his court) are sheer curtains of richly coloured and intricately detailed stained glass, which bathe the chapel in a kaleidoscope of extraordinary light.

The 15 windows depict biblical scenes, from **Genesis** (on the left as you enter the chapel) to the **Story of the Relics** (on the right). The **rose window**, features the story of the Apocalypse told in 86 panels of stained glass. Some 720 of the 1134 scenes depicted in the windows are the original stained glass – the oldest in Paris.

INFORMATION

☎ 01 53 40 60 97
🖥 www.monum.fr
✉ Palais de Justice, blvd du Palais, 1er
€ €6.10/4.10
🕐 9.30am-6pm Mar-Oct, 9am-5pm Nov-Feb
ℹ guided tours (in English) €6.10/4.10
Ⓜ Cité
♿ accessible
✗ Le Dauphin (p69)

DON'T MISS
- Medieval wooden statues of the apostles
- 75m spire made of cedar
- Window depicting the life of Moses
- Richly painted vaulting of the Lower Chapel

Built in just three years, Ste-Chapelle was consecrated in 1248. Conceived by Louis IX (St Louis) to house his collection of holy relics, it held the alleged Crown of Thorns and part of John the Baptist's skull (which was purchased at several times the cost of building the chapel). The relics were displayed on the wooden canopied platform in front of the altar, but the reliquary was destroyed during the Revolution and the relics relocated to Notre Dame.

The Gothic folk knew how to be enlightened with flair

LES ÎLES (5, C2 & D3)

The most romantic part of Paris, these two islands on the Seine have historically been the geographical, commercial, religious and political heart of the city. While no longer the centre of religious and political power, the island's monuments, bridges and quays are still Paris' most enigmatic attractions.

> **INFORMATION**
> Ⓜ Cité
> ♿ accessible
> ✖ Mon Vieil Ami (p77)

The larger of the two linked islands **Île de la Cité** (5, C2), is the historic and tourist centre of Paris. **Notre Dame** (5, C3; p9) is its prime attraction, but stunning **Ste-Chapelle** (5, C2; opposite) and the moving **Mémorial des Martyrs de la Déportation** (5, D3) are all worth exploring. Despite its name, the **Pont Neuf** or New Bridge (5, B2) is the oldest of the Seine's 37 bridges (which was built 1578–1604). Leading off Pont Neuf is one of the prettiest spots in Paris, the **Square du Vert Galant**, with wonderful Seine views.

> **DON'T MISS**
> - Secluded place Dauphine
> - Église St-Louis-en-l'Île
> - Daily flower market and Sunday bird market
> - Quayside *bouquinistes* (book stalls)
> - The view at night

With no tourist hotspots lining its enchanting streets, **Île St-Louis** (5, D6) is an oasis of calm and charm. The island's 17th-century stone houses, teahouses, boutiques and galleries make the island perfect for a romantic stroll. The area around **Pont St-Louis** (linking the two islands) and **Pont Louis-Philippe** is picture-postcard Paris, while Paris' best ice cream is sold at **Berthillon** (5, D3; 31 rue St-Louis en l'Île). Even its insignia is exquisite.

A glass-and-steel-free zone on Île de la Cité

JEAN-BERARD CARILLET

SACRÉ CŒUR & MONTMARTRE (4, D2)

Visible from many parts of the city, the immense **Basilique du Sacré Cœur** (Basilica of the Sacred Heart), sits perched on the summit of the **Butte de Montmartre** (Montmartre Hill, the highest point in Paris). While it looks much older, visitors are surprised to learn that the Basilica was only consecrated in 1919 as an act of contrition following

INFORMATION
- ✉ place du Parvis du Sacré Cœur, 18e
- Ⓜ Abbesses
- ♿ difficult
- ✕ La Table d'Anvers (p72)

JONATHAN SMITH

the humiliating Franco-Prussian war of 1870–1.

Taking the 234 spiralling steps to the basilica's dome affords one of Paris' most spectacular panoramas – which extends up to 30km on a clear day. Inside the basilica there's a massive mosaic of Christ in the chancel vault.

Surrounding the basilica, the Butte de Montmartre retains much of its bohemian village feel.

Headless on Montmartre

Saint Denis, patron saint of France, introduced Christianity to Paris in the 2nd century. He was beheaded by the Romans on the hill now named Montmartre (Martyr Hill); you'll often see statues of him holding his head under his arm (on Notre Dame's portal). This is often regarded as a reference to the legend of him running with his head in his hand after being beheaded.

In its twisting, narrow streets you'll find Paris' two surviving **windmills** (*moulins*; 4, C1), sole **vineyard** (4, D1; rue des Saules) and the legendary **Au Lapin Agile** (p89) nightclub.

While Van Gogh, Renoir, Picasso and Dalí once set up their easels in **place du Tertre** (4, D2) they've been spared the indignity of seeing the 'art' being sold there today, but the place still has loads of character.

For a walk around Montmartre, see p44.

JEAN-BERNARD CARILLET

Don't confuse Montmartre's *moulins* or you might get to see windmills of legs instead

MARAIS & PLACE DES VOSGES   (5, E2)

The Marais quarter is arguably Paris' most enchanting neighbourhood. Its pre-Revolution architecture and narrow streets complement the dozens of bars, boutiques and restaurants that have blossomed here in recent years. At its heart is an elegant square that is an essential stop in Paris.

In the early 1600s, Henri IV built the place Royal (now known as the **place des Vosges**), creating Paris' most chic residential district, with 36 symmetrical houses featuring ground-floor arcades, steep slate roofs and large dormer windows.

INFORMATION
- ✉ 3e & 4e
- Ⓜ St-Paul
- ♿ OK
- ✖ Chez Marianne (p70)

Be 'swamped' in fashion in the Marais

DON'T MISS
- Hôtel de Sully (p32)
- Felafel in the Jewish quarter
- Boutiques along rue Vieille du Temple (5, E1) & rue des Francs Bourgeois (5, E2)
- The view of place des Vosges from rue de Birague

Pre-Revolution place des Vosges

The central park that once echoed the sounds of jousting and duels, today reverberates with the noises of frolicking children. A great chance to admire one of the houses is by visiting the **Maison de Victor Hugo** (6 place des Vosges), where Hugo lived from 1832 to 1848.

When the surrounding marsh (*marais*) was drained wealthy aristocrats built grand *hôtels particuliers* (private mansions) nearby; these now house museums and government institutions, such as the **Musée Picasso** (p24).

After WWII, the Marais area became one of the most neglected in Paris and it wasn't until it was declared an historic monument in 1962 that it began to revive. The **Jewish quarter** around the rue des Rosiers and rue des Écouffes is lively, and the Marais has become the centre of Paris' vibrant gay community. For a walk around Marais, see (p42).

HÔTEL DES INVALIDES (3, C3)

The grand Hôtel des Invalides was built by Louis XIV in the 1670s as a residential village for up to 4000 *invalides* (disabled veterans), who were begging on Paris' streets. The courtyard, **Cour d'Honneur**, is used for military parades, overlooked by a statue of Napoleon.

Seen from behind the four-storey classical façade is the stunning **Église du Dôme** (Dome Church), so named for its glittering dome.

INFORMATION

- ☎ 01 44 42 37 72
- 🖳 www.invalides.org in French
- ✉ Esplanade des Invalides, 7e
- € tomb & museum €7/5
- 🕑 museum 10am-6pm (to 5pm Oct-Mar); Napoleon's tomb 10am-6.45pm mid-Jun–mid-Sep
- ⓘ guided 'themed' tours (book well ahead) ☎ 01 44 42 37 72
- Ⓜ Invalides
- ♿ accessible
- ✖ café

DON'T MISS

- The tomb of Napoleon's older brother, Joseph
- The tomb of WWI military leader, Marshal Foch
- The circular painting on the Dôme

One of the finest religious buildings built under Louis XIV, it was created between 1677 and 1735; the dome taking 27 years to finish. It was intended for the king's use and as a royal mausoleum, but became a mausoleum for military leaders.

Fulfilling Napoleon's wish to be buried on the banks of the Seine, the Église du Dôme is home to **Napoleon's tomb**. Napoleon's remains were moved here in 1861, 40 years after his death. Rather like a Russian *matryoshka* doll, Napoleon's body is encased in five coffins and a sarcophagus of red porphyry, displayed in an open crypt. The comprehensive **Musée de l'Armée** (p27) is also part of the complex.

A house for a king, a hospital for war veterans and a museum – this place is versatile

JEAN-BERNARD CARILLET

CIMETIÈRE DU PÈRE LACHAISE (2, H3)

With its tree-lined lanes, remarkable funerary sculpture, and prime position overlooking the city, this would still be a great place for a stroll even without the tombs of the rich and famous to distract you. Founded in 1804, this cemetery has expanded – it's still Paris' most fashionable address to be laid to rest.

Buried here are the composer Chopin; writers Molière, Apollinaire, Oscar Wilde, Balzac, Marcel Proust, Gertrude Stein (and Alice B Toklas) and Colette; artists David, Delacroix, Pissarro, Seurat and Modigliani; actors Sarah Bernhardt, Simone Signoret and Yves Montand; singer Édith Piaf; dancer Isadora Duncan; and those immortal 12th-century lovers **Abélard and Héloïse** (the oldest of the cemetery's one million residents). Those with a love of dire rock star poetry go to the nondescript grave of 1960s rock icon **Jim Morrison**, of the Doors, who died in Paris in 1971. Also notable is the **Mur des Fédérés** (Federalists' Wall), so named because of the 147 Communard insurgents lined up and shot here on 27 May 1871.

INFORMATION

- ☎ 01 55 25 82 10
- ✉ blvd de Ménilmontant, 20e
- € free
- 🕐 8am-6pm, from 8.30am Sat, from 9am Sun
- ℹ guided tours (in English) €9/6 3pm Sat
- Ⓜ Philippe Auguste
- ♿ difficult
- ✗ Le Zéphyr (p76)

Maps indicating the location of noteworthy graves are posted around the cemetery. Newsstands and kiosks sell more detailed maps.

Devilish Angels

Oscar Wilde's tomb features a Jacob Epstein sculpture of a winged angel, whose genitals were considered so obscene that they were hacked off and apparently used as a paperweight by the cemetery's director.

An angel would need more than wings to keep up with Oscar Wilde's wit

JEAN-BERNARD CARILLET

CHÂTEAU DE VERSAILLES (1, D2)

Louis XIV (1638–1715) was a ruler who led his life pursuing magnificence and the glorious Château de Versailles is a tribute to this obsession. The grandest and most famous chateau in France was the kingdom's political capital and the seat of the royal court from 1682 to 1789.

INFORMATION

- ☎ 01 30 83 78 00
- 🖳 www.chateauver sailles.fr
- ✉ Versailles, 23km from Paris
- € château €7.50, Grand/Petit Trianon €5; gardens €3 Apr-Oct, free other times except for concerts (Sat Jul-Aug, Sun Apr-Oct)
- ⌚ château 9am-5.30pm Tue-Sun (to 6.30pm May-Sep), gardens dawn-dusk
- ⓘ Audioguide, €4.50, guided visits 1/1½/2hrs €4/6/8 (book on arrival)
- ⓡ RER line C; SNCF from Gare St-Lazare
- ♿ reasonable access
- ✕ café

Let Them Eat Cake

On 5 October 1789 a mob of women protesting about bread shortages marched the 23km from Paris to Versailles. The much-reviled Marie-Antoinette escaped using a secret passage to her husband's bedroom, but the next day, both Louis XVI and his queen were dragged back to Paris. They never saw Versailles again.

After building started in the mid-1600s, Louis (the 'Sun King') pushed the 30,000 workers and kingdom's finances to the brink of collapse with his expensive tastes. The complex has four parts: the sumptuous 580m-long palace with innumerable wings, grand halls and plush bedchambers; the vast gardens, canals and pools west of the palace; and two smaller palaces, the Grand Trianon and Petit Trianon.

See the dazzling **Galeries des Glaces** (Hall of Mirrors), **Opéra Royal**, **Chapelle Royale** and the **Grand Appartement du Roi**, while the beautiful symmetrical palace gardens are worth a day's visit.

The Trianons are located in the the park's centre, about 1.5km from the palace itself. Nearby is the **Hameau de la Reine** (Queen's Hamlet), a mock village of thatched cottages built for Marie-Antoinette's amusement.

Even classical gods kick back and enjoy the vista from the chateau's grounds

JARDIN DU LUXEMBOURG (3, F5)

Paris' most popular park, the Luxembourg Gardens is 25 hectares of formal FrancoItalian-style terraces, chestnut groves, gardens and enchantingly Parisian leisure activities.

Napoleon dedicated the gardens to the children of Paris and he would approve of the whimsical fun

JONATHAN SMITH

INFORMATION

☎ 01 42 34 20 00

✉ blvd St-Michel, rue de Vaugirard, 6e

€ gardens free; boats/*carrousel*/marionettes/playgrounds/pony rides €2.75 per hr/1.15/3.70/2.20/2.30

⏱ 7.30am-9.30pm Apr-Oct, 8am-5pm Nov-Mar, marionettes 3-4pm Wed, Sat & Sun

Ⓜ Odéon

♿ OK

✕ Polidor (p75)

> **A Bird in the Hand**
> As a struggling writer with a huge appetite, Ernest Hemingway (when not having scored a dinner invitation) visited the gardens before heading home for dinner – not for a stroll, but to catch pigeons for cooking.

available for *les gosses* (the kids), from renting model sailing boats at the **Grand Bassin** (the octagonal pond) to cheering *guignol* (marionettes) at the **Théâtre du Luxembourg**. Next door, there's a modern **playground**, vintage swings and an old-time *carrousel* (merry-go-round) alongside pony rides.

In the northwest area of the gardens, chess and card games are held each afternoon. On the north side of the *théâtre* there are basketball and volleyball courts and intense games of *boules* (traditional bowls) in play.

Less active visitors can simply enjoy the vibrant floral displays (best in spring) or bone-up on their bee-keeping skills at the **apiary**. The ancient *verger* (orchard) contains 200 types of pear and apple trees.

The **Palais du Luxembourg** is at the park's northern edge, with the Italianate **Fontaine des Médicis** (1642) located nearby. The **Musée du Luxembourg** hosts art exhibitions from different regions of France.

JEAN-BERNARD CARILLET

Jardin du Luxembourg! Isn't this France?

MUSÉE NATIONAL DU MOYEN ÂGE (5, B3)

The Museum of the Middle Ages (often called the Musée de Cluny) is uniquely housed in the remains of the Gallo-Roman baths (dating from around AD 200) and the late-15th-century Hôtel de Cluny, once the home of the Abbots of Cluny. It's the city's finest example of medieval civil architecture in the city.

In an intriguing and intimate two-storey space you'll find one of the best collections of medieval statuary, illuminated manuscripts, arms, furnishings, and objects made from gold, ivory and enamel, as well as a display depicting aspects of everyday life during the Middle Ages.

> **INFORMATION**
> - ☎ 01 53 73 78 00
> - 🖥 www.musee-moyenage.fr
> - ✉ 6 place Paul Painlevé, 5e
> - € €5.50/4 (€4 for all on Sun)
> - 🕑 9.15am-5.45pm Wed-Mon
> - ℹ guided tours 11.45am Sat, 10am Sun except 1st Sun of month
> - Ⓜ Cluny-La Sorbonne
> - ♿ limited
> - ✖ Le Petit Pontoise (p78)

> **DON'T MISS**
> - 21 heads of the King of Judah (Gallery of the Kings)
> - Stained glass removed from Ste-Chapelle
> - Golden Rose of Basel, dating from 1330
> - Gorgeous jewellery and metal work

The highlight of the exhibits is the late-15th-century tapestries collectively known as *The Lady with the Unicorn*, hung in the 1st floor's room 13. Consisting of six exquisite pieces – five relating to the senses with the sixth being the enigmatic *To My Sole Desire*. A medieval garden and **Forêt de la Licorne** (Unicorn Forest) is laid out along blvd St-Germain inspired by the illustrations in the tapestries.

The remains of the *frigidarium* (cooling room) of the baths, with its 15m-high vaulted ceiling, is the setting for interesting mosaics and sculptural fragments.

JEAN-BERNARD CARILLET

Heads or tails?

MUSÉE RODIN (3, D4)

The renowned French sculptor, Auguste Rodin (1840–1917) lived and sculpted at this elegant state-owned *hôtel particulier*, **Hôtel Biron**, from 1908 until his death. Leaving his works to the nation upon his death, the government turned the *hôtel* into a museum. It's a treasure trove of his greatest works and one of Paris' most tranquil museums.

Artistic Hell

Rodin was commissioned to create a bronze door for the Musée des Arts Décoratifs by 1884, but when he died in 1917, the piece still remained his unfinished obsession. Inspired by Dante's *Divine Comedy,* the work eventually became known as *Gates of Hell* and studies that Rodin executed for it have become some of his best-known works including *The Thinker* and *The Kiss.*

INFORMATION
- ☎ 01 44 18 61 10
- 🖳 www.musee -rodin.fr
- ✉ 77 rue de Varenne, 7e
- € museum €5/3; gardens €1
- 🕙 9.30am-5.45pm Apr-Sep, to 4.45pm Oct-Mar
- Ⓜ Varenne
- ♿ limited
- 🍴 garden café

Rooms on two floors display bronze and marble sculptures, including casts of some of Rodin's most celebrated works: *The Hand of God, St John the Baptist, Balzac, Cathedral* and *The Kiss.* On display are works by Rodin's model, pupil and lover, Camille Claudel (1864–1943), whose gentle talent and fragile temperament was overwhelmed by Rodin's powerful personality.

The highlight of the museum is the splendid English-style **rose garden**, filled with shade trees and sculptures, including the original version of the work everyone comes to see, *The Thinker.* Other celebrated works in the garden are *The Burghers of Calais* and the unfinished *Gates of Hell,* which kept Rodin occupied for the last 33 years of his life.

Perfecting the body beautiful

JEAN-BERNARD CARILLET

MUSÉE PICASSO (5, E1)

Spain's loss was France's gain when Pablo Picasso (1881–1973) settled in Paris in 1904, as his family donated a quarter of his entire collection of drawings, engravings, paintings, ceramic works and sculptures to the French government in lieu of inheritance taxes. In 1985 the government inaugurated the Musée Picasso to display the collection. Although the works here aren't his most celebrated ones, the museum offers the most detailed overview

JEAN-BERNARD CARILLET

INFORMATION

☎ 01 42 71 25 21

🖳 www.musee
-picasso.fr

✉ 5 rue de Thorigny,
3e

€ €6.70/5.20

🕙 9.30am-6pm Wed-
Mon Apr-Sep, to
5.30pm Nov-Mar

Ⓜ St-Paul

♿ OK

🍴 summer café

DON'T MISS
- *Self-Portrait in Blue Period*
- *The Kiss*
- His own collection of Cézanne, Braque, Matisse and Degas works
- *Painter with Palette and Easel*
- *Two Women Running on the Beach*

of Picasso's oeuvre – particularly his playfulness and his resourceful use of materials.

The 200 paintings of the collection are arranged chronologically, from Picasso's early Blue and Rose periods to the flowering of Cubism and pieces from his later years. Roughly 3000 drawings and engravings give an insight into his artistic methods, while more than 100 ceramic works and sculptures demonstrate his mastery of a wide variety of media.

Tucked away in the Marais, the museum resides in the **Hôtel Salé**, a carefully restored mid-17th-century mansion.

Surrealism this way

JONATHAN SMITH

PARC DE LA VILLETTE (2, H1)

This futuristic park in the city's far-northeastern corner is a whimsical wonderland for kids and adults. Since 1993 its lawns have been enlivened by walkways, eccentric public furniture, themed gardens and *folies*, bright-red building-sculptures.

The park's main attraction is the enormous **Cité des Sciences et de l'Industrie**, an interactive

INFORMATION

☎ Parc 01 04 03 75 75; CSI 01 40 05 80 00; la Géode 01 40 05 79 99; Cinaxe 01 42 09 85 83; Cité de la Musique 01 44 84 44 84

▢ www.villette.com; www.lageode.fr; www.cite-sciences .fr (in French); www .cite-musique.fr

✉ 30 av Corentin-Cariou, 19e

€ depends on exhibits

🕐 Cinaxe 11am-5pm (5min films per 15mins); Cité de la Musique noon-6pm Tue-Sat, 10am-6pm Sun; CSI Tue-Sun 10am-6pm; Géode 10am 9pm (45min films per hr)

ⓘ varies with exhibit

Ⓜ Porte de la Villette

♿ OK

🍴 Café de la Musique

DON'T MISS

- Open-air cinema
- *Jardin des Frayeurs Enfantines* (Garden of Childhood Frights)
- *Argonaut* (a dry docked French submarine)
- Maison de la Villette (displays the site's history)
- Buried Bicycle sculpture

science museum, plus planetarium, **aquarium**, cinema and multimedia library. The Cité des Enfants is highly recommended and offers great activities for kids.

The adjacent **Géode** is a surreal 36m-diameter sphere with a mirrorlike surface that consists of thousands of highly polished, stainless-steel triangles. Inside, an Omnimax cinema has high resolution films projected onto a semispherical, 180° screen giving your peripheral vision a slice of the action. The **Cinaxe** is a 60-seat hydraulic cinema that moves in sync with the action on the screen.

The **Cité de la Musique** includes a concert hall as well as the National Conservatory of Dance and Music. There's a wonderful

JEAN-BERNARD CARILLET

Does the Géode foretell the future as well?

music museum, with over 4500 instruments from the 16th century onwards and infrared headsets enabling visitors to listen to audio extracts related to the instruments on show.

LA DÉFENSE (2, A1)

Given Paris' handsome historic centre, we can be grateful that La Défense is where Paris' big end of town grew. The concrete, glass and steel necessary to reflect corporate power is here – but executed with typically French flair. On the banks of the Seine, La Défense was one of the world's most ambitious urban construction projects, beginning in the late 1950s. The first main structure was the vaulted, triangular-shaped

DON'T MISS
- CNIT plus the Fiat, Manhattan and Elf office buildings
- Dôme IMAX cinema
- Musée de l'Automobile
- The garden, featuring works by Calder, Miró and Agam

INFORMATION
- ☎ 01 49 07 27 57 (La Grande Arche)
- 🖳 www.grandearche.com
- ✉ parvis de Défense
- € Grande Arche €7.50/6
- ☖ Grande Arche 10am-7pm
- ⓘ Info Défense ☎ 01 47 74 84 24, 15 place de la Défense, 10am-6pm (guides available)
- Ⓜ La Défense Grande Arche
- ♿ good

JEAN-BERNARD CARILLET

Centre des Nouvelles Industries et Technologies (CNIT), inaugurated in 1958 and rebuilt 30 years later. Today over 100 buildings are on-site and 14 of France's 20 largest corporations are housed here.

The most important structure of the site is the extraordinary **Grande Arche de la Défense**, designed by Danish architect Otto von Spreckelsen. This hollow cube of white Italian marble and glass measures 111m on each side – the hollow section is large enough to contain Notre Dame. One of Mitterrand's *grands travaux* (p31), it was opened on 14 July 1989, and forms the western terminus of the 8km-long **Grand Axe** (Great Axis), linking the Louvre's pyramid and the Arc de Triomphe. The structure symbolises a window open to the world, and is a modern echo of the Arc de Triomphe.

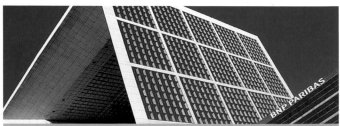

JONATHAN SMITH

No baroque baubles here

Sights & Activities

MUSEUMS

For more 'must-see' museums, see the Highlights chapter (p8), and Paris for Children (p39) and Quirky Paris (p38).

Musée Carnavalet (5, E2)
Inside two enchanting *hôtels particuliers* (private mansions), this museum shows Paris' history, including Neolithic artefacts and Marcel Proust's cork-lined bedroom! With over 140 rooms to visit, the chronologically arranged displays are a blessing and the temporary exhibitions are great.
☎ 01 44 59 58 58
🖳 www.paris.fr/musees/musee_carnavalet/ ✉ 23 rue de Sévigné, 3e
€ free, exhibitions €5.50/4 🕑 10am-5pm Tue-Sun Ⓜ St-Paul
♿ limited

Musée d'Art et d'Histoire (1, E2) A worthwhile detour on a visit to the Basilique de St-Denis (p34), this museum is in a restored 1625 Carmelite convent. There are poems and documents of St-Denis–born Surrealist Paul Éluard (1895–1952) plus religious art shown on the 1st floor.
☎ 01 42 43 05 10
✉ 22bis rue Gabriel Péri, St-Denis € €4/2
🕑 10am-5.30pm Wed-Mon, 2-6.30pm Sun
Ⓜ St-Denis-Basilique
♿ limited

Musée d'Art et d'Histoire du Judaïsme (5, D1)
Situated in the grand 17th-century Hôtel de St-Aignan in the heart of the Marais, this museum recounts the history of Jewish communities, emphasising France. Highlights include documents relating to the Dreyfus Affair and works by Chagall and Modigliani.
☎ 01 53 01 86 53
🖳 www.mahj.org
✉ 71 rue du Temple, 3e
€ €6.10/3.80 🕑 11am-6pm Mon-Fri, 10am-6pm Sun Ⓜ Arts et Métiers
♿ good

Musée de la Mode et du Textile (3, E3) Fashionistas flock to this history of fabrics, clothing and accessories from the 16th century to 20th-century icons such as works by Dior and Schiaparelli. The displays are themed and change a couple of times a year.
☎ 01 44 55 57 50
🖳 www.ucad.fr ✉ Palais du Louvre, 107 rue de Rivoli, 1er € €6/4.50 (incl Musée des Arts Décoratifs, p28) 🕑 11am-6pm Tue-Fri, 10am-6pm Sat & Sun Ⓜ Palais Royal
♿ OK

Musée de l'Armée (3, C4)
This museum is a must for military history buffs, with an absorbing section on WWII. The wartime footage may leave you teary-eyed, but the volume of weapons, flags and medals on show will make them glaze over. Sections are closed for renovation until late 2005.
☎ 01 44 42 37 72
🖳 www.invalides.org
✉ Hôtel National des Invalides, Esplanades des Invalides, 7e € €7/5.50 🕑 10am-6pm Apr-Sep, 10am-5pm Oct-Mar,

Arm yourself for the war stories in here

JEAN-BERNARD CARILLET

These accoutrements at Musée des Arts Décoratifs glittered from necks across the ages

closed 1st Mon of month
M Invalides ♿ good

Musée de l'Homme (3, A3)
The Museum of Mankind
shows a fascinating view of
human evolution, anthropol-
ogy and culture, plus exhibits
relating to Africa, Asia, Europe, the Arctic, the Pacific,
and the Americas. Steady
yourself for the population
growth display connected to
UN statistics.
☎ 01 44 05 72 72
🖥 www.mnhn.fr

GO-Fast Pass
If you plan to visit multiple museums and monuments over just a few days, or want to avoid long
queues, buy a **Carte Musées-Monuments** (€18/36/
54 for 1/3/5 days), from major metro stations, par-
ticipating museums and tourist offices.

Retro metro

in French ✉ Palais de
Chaillot, 17 place du
Trocadéro, 16e € €7/3
🕑 9am-5pm Wed-Mon
M Trocadéro ♿ OK

**Musée des Arts
Décoratifs (3, E3)** This
collection has furniture,
jewellery and ceramic and
glassware *objets d'art* from
the Middle Ages to recent
times. Areas may be closed
for renovations until 2006.
☎ 01 44 55 57 50
🖥 www.ucad.fr ✉ Pal-
ais du Louvre, 107 rue de
Rivoli, 1er 🕑 11am-6pm
Tue-Sun, 10am-6pm Sat
& Sun € €6/4.50 (incl
entry to other museums
in the Palais du Louvre)
M Palais Royal ♿ good

**Musée des Arts et
Métiers (3, H2)** This
Arts and Crafts Museum,
Europe's oldest museum of
science and technology in
Europe, plots an engaging
history of machines and

instruments. The museums' layout across three floors is easily navigable. The most notable exhibit is Foucault's original pendulum from 1855, with which he proved that the world turns on its axis.
☎ 01 53 01 82 20
🖳 www.arts-et-metiers.net in French
✉ 60 rue Réaumur, 3e
€ €6.50/4.50 ☽ 10am-6pm Tue-Sun, to 9.30pm Thu Ⓜ Arts et Métiers ♿ good

Musée Édith Piaf (2, H3)
Die-hard fans of the 'little sparrow' won't regret having to book ahead to visit this lovingly assembled museum in Belleville where she was born and began her career. Almost as tiny as the iconic chanteuse herself, the museum displays memorabilia, recordings and video.
☎ 01 43 55 52 72 ✉ 5 rue Crespin du Gast, 11e
€ by donation ☽ 1-6pm Mon-Thu Ⓜ Ménilmontant

Musée Guimet des Arts Asiatiques (3, A3) Europe's most outstanding museum of Asian treasures features sculptures, paintings, *objets d'art* and religious articles from Afghanistan, India, Nepal, Pakistan, Tibet, Cambodia, China, Japan and Korea. The striking collection of 250 Buddhist paintings and sculptures is situated at 19 av d'Iéna. Be sure not to miss the tranquil Japanese garden.
☎ 01 56 52 53 00
🖳 www.museeguimet.fr
✉ 6 place d'Iéna, 19

Just Relax
While the large *luxe* hotels have great spas, these bathhouses offer a more interesting experience. The **Hammam de la Mosquée de Paris** (3, H6, ☎ 01 43 31 18 14; 39 rue Geoffroy-St-Hilaire, 5e; baths/massages €14/9.50; ☽ 10am-9pm; men Tue & Sun, women other days; Ⓜ place Monge) is where you step out of the West and into the East in this wonderfully exotic bathhouse at Paris' Grand Mosque. Relax in the public baths or experience a traditional massage. See (p79) for restaurant details.

The **Les Bains du Marais** (5, D1; ☎ 01 42 61 02 02; www.lesbainsdumarais.com in French; 31-33 rue des Blancs Manteaux, 4e; hammam/30min massage €28/28; ☽ women 11am-8pm Mon, to 11pm Tue, 10am-7pm Wed; men 11am-11pm Thu, 10am-8pm Fri & Sat; mixed 7pm-midnight Wed, 11am-11pm Sun; Ⓜ Hôtel de Ville) is a comfortable, modern bath complex providing traditional Moroccan glove massages (*gommages*), essential oil massages, shampoos, facials, pedicures as well as henna tattoos.

av d'Iéna, 16e € €7/5 ☽ 10am-6pm Wed-Mon Ⓜ Iéna ♿ OK

Musée National des Arts et Traditions Populaires (2, B2) The National Museum of Popular Arts and Traditions has displays regarding rural France before and during the Industrial Revolution. This antidote to Paris' museums about royalty shows how the other half – the rural poor – lived, worked and played in preindustrial France.
☎ 01 44 17 60 00
🖳 www.culture.fr /culture/atp/mnatp ✉ 6 av du Mahatma Gandhi, 16e € €3.80/2.60 ☽ 9.30am-5.15pm Wed-Mon Ⓜ Les Sablons ♿ OK

Musée National Eugène Delacroix (5, A2) The key artist of French Romanticism moved to this studio in the leafy neighbourhood while he painted the murals in nearby Église St-Sulpice (p34). You'll see some of Delacroix's (1798 1863) more intimate works such as *An Unmade Bed*, a selection of his Moroccan paintings, sketches as well as a selection of his personal possessions. Major paintings are on exhibition at the Louvre (p11) and the Musée d'Orsay (p12).
☎ 01 44 41 86 50
🖳 www.musee-de lacroix.fr ✉ 6 place de Furstemberg, 6e
€ €4/2.60 ☽ 9.30am-5pm Wed-Mon Ⓜ Mabillon ♿ limited

GALLERIES

Espace Montmartre Salvador Dalí (4, D2)
Displaying sculptures, lithographs and illustrations by the famous Spanish Surrealist and ceaseless self-promoter, this gallery lacks well-known works by Dalí (1904–89), but there's a dramatic 'sound-and-light' show atmosphere.
☎ 01 42 64 40 10
🖥 www.dali-espace montmartre.com ✉ 9-11 rue Poulbot, 14e € €7/6
🕐 10am-6.30pm (to 9pm Jul-Aug)
Ⓜ Abbesses 🦽 limited

Fondation Cartier pour l'Art Contemporain (2, E5) Founded in 1984 by the famous watch and jewellery company, this stunning transparent glass-and-metal space showcases contemporary art, design, installations and perform-ance pieces. It hosts several exhibitions a year, with designers and artists asked to push their creativity past their genre or industry restrictions.
☎ 01 42 18 56 50
🖥 www.fondation .cartier.fr ✉ 261 blvd Raspail, 6e € €6.50/4.50
🕐 noon-8pm; Nomad Soirée (live art perform-ance) 8.30pm Thu
Ⓜ Raspail 🦽 OK

Maison Européenne de la Photographie (5, E2)
Housed in an 18th-century *hôtel particulier*, the gallery focusses on photography from the 1950s onwards, using Robert Frank's influential *The Americans* as a starting point. Iconic photographers are represented and there's a great Polaroid gallery and frequent temporary exhibitions.

☎ 01 44 78 75 00
🖥 www.mep-fr.org
✉ 5-7 rue de Fourcy, 4e € €6/3 🕐 11am-7.45pm Wed-Sun
Ⓜ St-Paul 🦽 OK

Musée d'Art Moderne de la Ville de Paris (3, B3)
While the Centre Pompidou (p13) might have more high-profile works, early-20th-century artists such as Dufy (including his enor-mous *The Spark of Life*) and Matisse *(The Dance)* make this museum a rewarding experience. The museum is closed for renovations until late 2005.
☎ 01 53 67 40 00
🖥 www.paris-france .org ✉ 11 av du Prési-dent Wilson, 16e € €7/5 (free before 1pm Sun)
🕐 10am-5.30pm (to 7pm Sat & Sun) Ⓜ léna 🦽 good

Musée de l'Orangerie (3, D3) The collection's highlight is Monet's aston-ishing *Water Lilies* – eight huge panels conceived for the oval basement rooms of this former Tuileries greenhouse. It is closed for renovation until 2006.
☎ 01 42 97 48 16
✉ Jardin des Tuileries, 1er € €4.60/3.05
🕐 9.45am-5.15pm Wed-Mon Ⓜ Concorde 🦽 OK

Musée Gustave Moreau (3, F2) Housed in what was once Moreau's (1826–98) apartment and studio, the two-storey museum is crammed with 4800 paint-ings, drawings and sketches

Musée Jacquemart-André – an absolute treasure trove

by this significant Symbolist artist. Moreau's obsession with mythology and religion gives his work a dreamlike quality that significantly influenced the Surrealist movement that followed.
☎ 01 48 74 38 50 ⊠ 14 rue de la Rochefoucauld, 9e € €4/2.60 ⌚ 10am-12.45pm & 2-5.15pm Wed-Mon Ⓜ Trinité ♿ limited

Musée Jacquemart-André (3, C1) This sumptuous residence was purpose-built to house the collection that Edouard André and his portraitist wife Nélie Jacquemart were amassing in the mid-19th century. The collection is as equally stunning as their mansion – Rembrandt, van Dyck, Botticelli and Tintoretto are just some of the artists whose works adorn the walls. The Jardin d'Hiver (Winter Garden), with its double-helix marble staircase, is definitely worth seeing.
☎ 01 42 89 04 91 ⌨ www.musee-jacquemart-andre.com ⊠ 158 blvd Haussmann, 8e € €8.50/6.50 ⌚ 10am-6pm Ⓜ St-Philippe du Roule ♿ OK

Musée Marmottan – Claude Monet (2, B3) The largest collection of works by Claude Monet (1840–1926) contains his *Impression: Sunrise*, from which the impressionist movement derived its name, and pieces from the *Water Lilies* series. There are exquisite 13th-century Wildenstein illuminated manuscripts and paintings

by Gauguin and Renoir.
☎ 01 42 24 07 02 ⌨ www.marmottan .com ⊠ 2 rue Louis-

Boilly, 16e € €6.50/4 ⌚ 10am-5.30pm Tue-Sun Ⓜ La Muette ♿ OK

The Grander Scheme of Things

Paris is a city overflowing with historic monuments built by kings and…François Mitterrand. The French President from 1981 until 1995, Mitterrand served with one eye on the legacy he would leave behind – the concrete, glass and steel of his *grands travaux* (grand projects). This was an ambitious public works programme which locals knew was necessary, but where the results divided popular opinion. Most of the grand projects were controversial when commissioned and all have had at least some teething problems. Still, all are worth visiting:

- **Bibliothèque Nationale de France François Mitterrand** (p32)
- **Grand Louvre project** (p11), part of the Louvre
- **Grande Arche La Defense** (p26)
- **Institut du Monde Arabe** (p32)
- **Opéra Bastille** (p33)
- **Parc De La Villette**, including the **Cité des Sciences et de l'Industrie** and the **Cité de la Musique** (p25)

Reflect on the Institut du Monde Arabe (p32)

NOTABLE BUILDINGS

Bibliothèque Nationale de France François Mitterrand (2, G5)

Dominique Perrault's contentious design of four L-shaped towers resembling open books has proven to be visually arresting. While Perrault was busy explaining the design's metaphors, others were questioning the wisdom of storing books and historical documents in 79m-high glass towers. A complex, expensive shutter system solved that problem, but bookworms and researchers sit in artificially lit basement halls built around a 'forest courtyard'.
☎ 01 53 79 49 49
🖳 www.bnf.fr ✉ 11 Quai François Mauriac, 13e € 2-day pass €4.50 🕑 10am-8pm Tue-Sat, noon-7pm Sun Ⓜ Quai de la Gare 🕭 good

Conciergerie (5, C2)

This fairy-tale building is part of the Palais de Justice complex and was a royal palace in the 14th century. During the Revolution, the

Storm the Opéra Bastille

building became a prison for those people, including Marie-Antoinette, who were waiting to appear before the Revolutionary Tribunal. The Gothic **Salle des Gens d'Armes** (Cavalrymen's Hall) dates from the 14th century and exemplifies Rayonnant Gothic style.
☎ 01 53 73 78 50 ✉ 1 Quai de l'Horloge, 1er € €7.50/5.50, with Ste-Chapelle (p14) €10.40/7.40 🕑 9.30am-6.30pm summer, 10am-5pm winter Ⓜ Cité 🕭 limited

Hôtel de Sully (5, E2)

Built in 1642 and fully restored in the early 1970s, the Hôtel de Sully is a superb example of an aristocratic mansion. Worth noting are the late Renaissance-style courtyards adorned with bas-reliefs of the seasons and the elements. Today it has the **Centre des Monuments Nationaux** (Monum; ☎ 01 44 61 20 00; www.monum.fr; 🕑 9am-12.45pm & 2-6pm Mon-Thu, 9am-12.45pm & 2-5pm Fri), the body responsible for many of France's historical monuments, as well as the **Mission du Patrimoine Photographique** (☎ 01 42 74 47 75; € €4/2.50; 🕑 10am-6.30pm Tue-Sun), which holds photographic exhibits.
☎ 01 44 61 20 00
✉ 62 rue St-Antoine, 4e € free except for exhibitions 🕑 garden 9am-7pm; library 10am-

6pm Tue-Sat Ⓜ St-Paul 🕭 limited

Hôtel de Ville (5, D2)

Paris' city hall was rebuilt in the neo-Renaissance style and completed in 1882 after having been gutted during the Paris Commune (1871, p104). The ornate façade is decorated with statues of noteworthy Parisians. The charming place de l'Hôtel de Ville, becomes an ice-skating rink in winter – a radical departure from the hangings, burnings and executions of its long past.
☎ 01 42 76 50 49
🖳 www.paris.fr
✉ place de l'Hôtel de Ville, 4e € guided tours free (book ahead) Ⓜ Hôtel de Ville 🕭 limited

Institut du Monde Arabe (E, H5)

Established to promote cultural exchange between the Arab world and the West, the Institute of the Arab World is housed in Jean Nouvel's stunning building that blends modern and traditional Arab and Western elements. The **museum**, spread over three floors, displays 9th- to 19th-century Arabian art and artisanship, as well as astronomical instruments and other fields of endeavour which had been ground-breaking at the time. The most unique feature of this building is its thousands of *mouche-arabies* (photo-electrically sensitive apertures built into the glass walls),

inspired by the traditional latticed wooden windows.
☎ 01 40 51 38 38
💻 www.imarabe.org
✉ 1 rue des Fossés St-Bernard, 5e € museum €4/3 ⏰ 10am-6pm Tue-Fri, 10am-7pm Sat & Sun Ⓜ Cardinal Lemoine ♿ OK

Opéra Bastille (3, F3)

Paris' huge 'second' opera house was opened on 14 July 1989, the 200th anniversary of the storming of the Bastille. A controversial *grands travaux* (see p31) construction, critics slammed the design, acoustics were considered poor and the building's limestone façade began to crack in 1991. After one slab fell off, the building was netted and lawyers still argue about who'll foot the repair bill. See p92 for concert details.
☎ 01 40 01 19 70
💻 www.opera-de-paris.fr ✉ 2-6 place de la Bastille, 11e € 1¼hr guided tours €10/8 Ⓜ Bastille ♿ good

Palais de Chaillot (3, A3)

Originally constructed for the 1937 Exposition Universelle (World Fair) held in Paris, this neoclassically styled *palais* looks onto Jardins du Trocadéro, the Seine and the Eiffel Tower. It accommodates the **Cinémathèque Française** (p88) film library, the **Musée de l'Homme** (p28) and the **Musée de la Marine** (Maritime Museum; ☎ 01 53 65 69 53; 💻 www.musee-marine.fr).

> ### Art Nouveau Metro
>
> The glorious Art Nouveau metro entrances in Paris are the work of Hector Guimard, who designed them between 1898 and 1905. Born in Lyon, he studied decorative arts and architecture in Paris and after visiting Hotel Tassel in Brussels (one of the first Art Nouveau buildings) he radically changed direction with his work. With his commission to design the metro entrances, his curvilinear lines and flourishes became synonymous with Art Nouveau style. While most of the complete Art Nouveau entrances have disappeared, the best ones to see are at **Porte Dauphine** (2, C3) and **place des Abbesses** (p35).

✉ place du Trocadéro, 16e ⏰ 10am-5pm Ⓜ Trocadéro ♿ OK

Palais Garnier (3, E2)

Hosting more ballet than opera these days (p93), this lavish opera house was designed by 35-year-old Charles Garnier 1860 to showcase Napoleon III's Second Empire. It's a distinctive monument with a breathtakingly opulent interior. Chagall painted the auditorium ceiling in 1964 (thankfully a false ceiling protects the original).
☎ 01 40 01 22 63
💻 www.opera-de-paris.fr ✉ place de l'Opéra, 9e € €6/4, guided tours €10/9 ⏰ 10am-5pm Ⓜ Opéra ♿ limited

Panthéon (3, G5)

Commissioned by Louis XV in 1744, this domed Parisian landmark was designed by Jacques-Germain Soufflot and wasn't completed until 1789. Given the revolutionary times, it was quickly repurposed into the Panthéon, a temple to the nation rather than to religion and designated the final resting place of France's 'great men' – Voltaire, Jean Jacques Rousseau, Victor Hugo and Marie Curie (the first woman to gain admittance).
☎ 01 44 32 18 00
💻 www.monum.fr ✉ place du Panthéon, 5e € €7/4.50 ⏰ 9.30am-6.30pm Apr-Sep, 10am-6.15pm Oct-Mar Ⓜ Cardinal Lemoine

Tour Montparnasse

(3, D6) Once Europe's tallest office block and still its ugliest, this steel and smoked-glass monolith has views of Paris from its 56th-floor indoor observatory. From the lift, hike up the stairs to the open-air terrace on the 59th floor.
☎ 01 45 38 52 56
💻 www.tourmontparnasse56.com ✉ rue de l'Arrivée, 15e € €8.20/7/5.60 ⏰ 9.30am-11.30pm Apr-Sep, 9.30am-10.30pm Sun-Thu, 9.30am-11pm Fri & Sat Oct-Mar Ⓜ Montparnasse Bienvenüe

PLACES OF WORSHIP

Basilique de Saint Denis (1, E2) Built over the tomb of St Denis, the first Bishop of Paris, this was the burial place for most French kings and queens from Dagobert I (r 629–39) to Louis XVIII (r 1814–24). The single-towered basilica, begun in 1135, was the forerunner of Gothic style and the tombs are one of Europe's paramount collections of funerary sculpture.
☎ 01 48 09 83 54
🖳 www.monum.fr
✉ 1 rue de la légion d'Honneur, St-Denis
🕐 10am-6.15pm Mon-Sat, noon-6.15pm Sun Apr-Sep, to 5.15pm Oct-Mar Ⓜ St-Denis-Basilique ♿ limited

Église St-Étienne du Mont (3, G6) Built between 1492 and 1655, this charming church combines various styles, with the Renaissance-era carved rood screen (1535) the item of most interest. In the nave's

Gothic Église St-Eustache

southeastern corner is a highly decorated reliquary containing the finger of Ste-Geneviève, the patron saint of Paris.
✉ place Ste-Geneviève, 5e 🕐 noon-7.30pm Mon, 8am-7.30pm Tue-Fri, 8am noon & 2-7.30pm Sat, 9am-noon & 2-7.30pm Sun Ⓜ Cardinal Lemoine ♿ OK

Église St-Eustache (3, G3) This historically significant and beautiful church was built between 1532 and 1640; it's Gothic in structure with early Renaissance aspects. Louis XIV celebrated his first communion and Liszt and Berlioz premiered new works here. The church is renowned for its choral and organ music, driven by the massive 8000 pipe organ. The website lists recital times.
☎ 01 42 36 31 05
🖳 www.st-eustache .org ✉ place du Jour, 1er 🕐 9am-7.30pm Ⓜ Les Halles ♿ OK

Église St-Germain des Prés (5, A2) Dating back to 542, this is the city's oldest existing church. Its main structure is from the 11th century. The Chapelle de St-Symphorien (to the entrance's right), is from the original abbey and is the resting place of St Germanus (AD 496–576), Paris' first bishop.
✉ place St-Germain des Prés, 6e 🕐 8am-7pm Mon-Sat, 9am-8pm Sun Ⓜ St-Germain des Prés ♿ OK

Église St-Séverin (5, C3) This flamboyant Gothic-style church was built between the 13th and 16th centuries. Take note of the spiral stonework of the double ambulatory (circular aisle) and the gargoyles outside.
✉ 1 rue des Prêtres-St-Séverin, 5e 🕐 11am-7.30pm Mon-Sat, 9am-8.30pm Sun Ⓜ St-Michel ♿ OK

Église St-Sulpice (5, A3) Several architects worked on this commanding church over 134 years, which explains the mismatched towers. Heading through the elegant Italianate façade you'll see Delacroix's vivid murals including *Jacob Wrestling with the Angel*. The 17th-century church is also known for its organ music.
✉ place St-Sulpice, 6e 🕐 8am-7pm Ⓜ St-Sulpice ♿ OK

Mosquée de Paris (3, H6) This exotic slice of the Maghreb in the heart of the Latin Quarter was built in the ornate Hispano-Moorish style in the 1920s, with serene courtyards and pink-marble fountains inspired by Alhambra. There is a central mosque, a *salon de thè* (tearoom), restaurant (p79) and a traditional Turkish *hammam* (p29).
☎ 01 45 35 97 33
✉ place du Puits-de-l'Ermite, 5e € €2.30/1.50 🕐 9am-noon, 2-6pm, Sat-Thu Ⓜ Place Monge ♿ limited

PLACES & SPACES

Place de Furstemberg
(5, A2) Tucked in behind Église St-Germain des Prés, this tiny square pulsates on summer evenings, when magnolias perfume the air and buskers serenade lovers under the old-fashioned streetlamps.

✉ **place de Furstemberg, 6e** Ⓜ **St-Germain des Prés**

Place de la Bastille
(5, F3) While Bastille Day (14 July) is a national holiday in France , the prison that the revolutionary mob stormed in 1789 has been replaced with a busy traffic roundabout. The 52m-high Colonne de Juillet (July Column) was erected in 1833 as a memorial for the July Revolution of 1830 and was later consecrated as a memorial to the February Revolution victims of 1848 (p104).

✉ **place de la Bastille, 11e** Ⓜ **Bastille**

Place de la Concorde
(3, D3) Paris' largest square was initially named place Louis XV and was completed in 1775. Named place de la Révolution in 1793, it reverberated to the sound of the guillotine; Louis XVI was one of the first 1000 victims to meet the blade in the next two years. After the Reign of Terror, the square was then given the conciliatory name of Concorde. The 3300-year-old, 23m pink granite obelisk in the centre of the square was given to France in 1831 and once stood in the Temple of Ramses

at Thebes (modern-day Luxor).

✉ **place de la Concorde, 8e** Ⓜ **Concorde**

Place de l'Hôtel de Ville
(5, D2) Since the Middle Ages this fountain-and-lamp-adorned square has been the venue for many Parisian celebrations, rebellions, book burnings and public executions. It's atmospheric at night, especially when there's an ice-skating rink in winter.

✉ **place de l'Hôtel de Ville, 1er** Ⓜ **Hôtel de Ville**

Place des Abbesses
(4, C3) This bustling square has one of the last Art Nouveau metro entrances (p33). The streets surrounding it offer interesting shopping.

✉ **place des Abbesses, 18e** Ⓜ **Abbesses**

Place Vendôme (3, E2)
Home to some of Paris' most exclusive boutiques and the Hôtel Ritz (p97) is the elegant, octagonal place Vendôme. Completed

Place Vendôme, very ritzy

in 1721, it's where Napoleon married Josephine (No 3) and Chopin died (No 12). In the centre, the 43.5m-tall Colonne Vendôme consists of a stone core wrapped in a 160m-long bronze spiral that's made from 1250 Austrian and Russian cannons captured by Napoleon.

✉ **place Vendôme, 1er** Ⓜ **Tuileries**

The Princess & the Memorial
The **place de l'Alma** (3, B3; Ⓜ Alma-Marceau) is nondescript, but on 31 August 1997 in the underpass parallel to the Seine, Diana, Princess of Wales, was killed in a car accident, with her companion, Dodi Fayed, and their chauffeur, Henri Paul. The bronze Flame of Liberty to the east, a replica of the one topping the torch of the Statue of Liberty, became an unofficial memorial to Diana and was decorated with flowers, photographs, graffiti and personal notes. It was cleaned up in 2002, but tourists still visit and leave flowers for the 'people's princess'.

PARKS & PROMENADES

Bois de Boulogne (2, A4)
Inspired by London's Hyde Park, these Haussmann-designed woods on the western edge of the city boast lakes, lawns, forests, flower gardens, meandering paths, cycling trails and *belle époque* (early-20th-century) cafés. Have a picnic, hire a bike or rowing boat, or stroll through the beautiful Parc de Bagatelle (2, D2). Those with kids should make a beeline for the Jardin d'Acclimatation (p39).
☽ 24hr (avoid after dark) Ⓜ Porte Dauphine ♿ ⚦

Bois de Vincennes (2, J5)
These vast gardens in the southeastern part of the city are popular for its lakes, a zoo, bike paths and Buddhist centre. Lovers of all things horticultural will enjoy the **Parc Floral de Paris** (⌨ www.parcfloral deparis.com). The park is also host to Frances' largest funfair, the Foire du Trône, in April and May, as well

as the turreted, medieval Château de Vincennes.
☎ 01 48 08 31 20
€ park free ☽ park dawn-dusk; château 10am-5pm, to 6pm summer Ⓜ Château de Vincennes Ⓡ RER Nogent-sur-Marne ♿

Canal St-Martin (3, J2)
Built between 1806 and 1825 to shortcut a loop in the Seine, these days the canal has fashionable cafés and boutiques lining its parallel streets. The shaded towpaths afford a romantic stroll along the canal's 4.5km length – especially at night – and the streets are closed to traffic on Sunday afternoons making the area popular with bike riders and inline skaters.
Ⓜ République, Jaurés, Stalingrad

Cimetière du Montparnasse (3, E6) While not as famous as Cimetière du Père Lachaise (p19), this serene cemetery houses some high-profile

residents. Intellectual existentialists Simone de Beauvoir and Jean-Paul Sartre put their minds to rest here. The most moving monument here is Constantin Brancusi's intriguing sculpture of a couple entwined, *The Kiss*.
☎ 01 44 10 86 50 ✉ 3 blvd Edgar Quinet, 14e ☽ 8am-6pm Mon-Fri, 8.30am-6pm Sat, 9am-6pm Sun mid-Mar–early Nov, to 5.30pm early Nov–mid-Mar Ⓜ Edgar Quinet

Jardin des Plantes (3, H6)
Founded in 1626 as a medicinal herb garden for Louis XIII, these small botanical gardens are delightfully informal. The Jardin d'Hiver (winter garden) and Jardin Alpin (alpine garden), tropical greenhouses and a small menagerie (zoo) await, as well as the fascinating Grande Galerie de l'Evolution (part of the Musée National d'Histoire Naturelle).
☎ 01 40 79 30 00
⌨ www.mnhn.fr ✉ 57 rue Cuvier, 5e € Jardin d'Hiver/ménagerie €2.30/6 ☽ park 8am-5.30pm; Jardin d'Hiver 1-5pm Mon & Wed-Fri, 1-6pm Sat & Sun Apr-Sep, 1-5pm Wed-Sun Oct-Mar; Jardin Alpin 8-11am & 1.30-5pm Mon-Fri Apr-Sep; ménagerie 9am-6pm Mon-Sat, to 6.30pm Sun Apr-Sep, 9am-5pm Mon-Sat, to 5.30pm Sun Oct-Mar Ⓜ Gare d'Austerlitz ♿ limited ⚦

Stroll, saunter or stride through Promenade Plantée (p37)

JEAN-BERNARD CARILLET

A production line of pedestrians at Parc André Citroën

Jardin des Tuileries (3, E3) This formal 28-hectare garden was opened in the 16th century, and was once Paris' most fashionable place to promenade. Stretching from the Louvre to place de la Concorde, its ponds, hedges and gravel paths are almost identical to the layout designed by royal gardener, André Le Nôtre.
☽ 7am-7.30pm late Sep–late-Mar, to 9pm late Mar–late Sep Ⓜ Tuileries ⅗ good

Parc André Citroën (2, C5) Named after the engineer who brought Henry Ford's mass production methods to France, this park is a tribute to André Citroën's enquiring mind and innovative ideas. Built on the banks of the Seine on the site of a former Citroën manufacturing plant, it features a series of thematic 'spaces' – the 'white garden', the 'black garden' and the whimsical 'restless garden'.
✉ rue Balard, 15e
☽ dawn-6pm Mon-Fri, 9am-6pm Sat & Sun
Ⓜ Balard ⅗ good

Parc des Buttes Chaumont (2, H2) A surprisingly hilly park located in northeast Paris, this former quarry was transformed by Baron Haussmann in the 1860s. It offers a huge lake, forested slopes, hidden grottoes, artificial waterfalls and unsurpassed views of Paris. Kids will love the puppet shows and donkey rides.
☎ 01 40 36 41 32 ✉ rue Armand Carrel, 19e

☽ 7am-9pm, to 11pm summer Ⓜ Buttes Chaumont ⅗ limited 🚲

Promenade Plantée (2, H4) This former railway line has been converted into a 4.5km elevated walkway that leads from the Bastille to the Bois de Vincennes, offering wonderful vistas. The tree- and flower-lined *coulée verte* (green strip) is used for jogging, while below the fashionable shops and ateliers of the viaduct are excellent for window-shopping.
🖥 www.promenade -plantee.org ✉ av Daumesnil btwn Opéra Bastille & Porte Dorée, 12e Ⓜ Bastille

---

Roll with It

Inline skaters should take the opportunity to join in one of the two so-called *Randonnées en Roller* (Skating Rambles) organised weekly throughout the year, attracting up to 10,000 participants. Skaters take back the streets (legally!) and it's a fun way to see Paris.

The **Pari Roller Ramble** (3, D6; ☎ 01 43 36 89 81; www.pari-roller.com; 14e; Ⓜ Montparnasse Bienvenüe) leaves place Raoul Dautry, located between gare Montparnasse and Tour Montparnasse, at 10pm Friday, returning at 1am. It's suited to skaters with reasonable ability. The family-oriented **Rollers & Coquillages Ramble** (☎ 01 44 54 07 44; www .rollers-coquillages.org; ☽ 2.30pm departure, returns 5.30pm Sun) leaves from blvd Bourdon, 4e, near place de la Bastille (3, J4; Ⓜ Bastille).

You can hire gear from **Bike 'n' Roller** (3, C3; ☎ 01 45 50 38 27; 38 rue Fabert, 7e; half-/full-day €9/12; ☽ 10am-8pm Mon-Sat, 10am-6.30pm Sun; Ⓜ Invalides). It has bicycles, *rollers* (inline skates), *quads* (roller skates) and *trottinettes* (scooters) for rent. Elbow/knee guards cost €1/1.50.

QUIRKY PARIS

Catacombes de Paris

(2, E5) In 1785 a grisly operation began to transfer exhumed bones from Paris' crowded cemeteries to tunnels of three disused quarries. One of those tunnels is now a macabre museum where millions of Parisians' bones and skulls are stacked in 1.6km of underground corridors. It's rivetting, but not for the squeamish or claustrophobic.
☎ 01 43 22 47 63 ✉ 1 place Denfert Rochereau, 14e € €5/3.30 ⏲ 2-4pm Tue-Fri, 9-11am & 2-4pm Sat & Sun Ⓜ Denfert Rochereau

Musée de la Poupée

(5, D1) A delicate museum strictly for doll lovers, there's over 500 pairs of glass eyes seemingly watching your every move. Scenes are arranged to represent Paris through the centuries and there's a doll 'hospital' and a shop.
☎ 01 42 72 73 11 ✉ Impasse Berthaud (nr 22 rue Beaubourg), 3e € €6/4 ⏲ 10am-6pm Tue-Sun Ⓜ Rambuteau ♿ OK ♨

Musée de l'Érotisme

(4, B3) Perfectly positioned in peepshow Pigalle, this museum boasts seven floors of exotic erotica. Barely a continent or community has been spared this homage to humankind getting stimulated, sated and impregnated. Once you've becomed bored looking at phalluses and fertility symbols, check out

Get the feeling you're being watched? Catacombes de Paris

the stunned silences and nervous laughter of other museumgoers.
☎ 01 42 58 28 73 🖥 www.eroticmuseum.com ✉ 72 blvd de Clichy, 18e € €7/5 ⏲ 10am-2am Ⓜ Blanche ♿ limited

Musée des Égouts de Paris

(3, B3) This 'breath-taking' working sewer museum offers you the questionable experience of having raw sewage flow beneath your feet as you walk through 480m of odoriferous tunnels, while learning about the development of Paris' waste-water disposal system.
☎ 01 53 68 27 81 ✉ 93 Quai d'Orsay, 7e € €3.80/2.30 ⏲ 11am-6pm Sat-Wed May-Sep, 11am-5pm Sat-Wed Oct-Apr Ⓜ Pont de l'Alma

Musée Grévin

(3, F1) This waxworks museum in the atmospheric passage Jouffroy, features plenty of 20th-century figures and historical French figures that will test the memory of all Francophiles. Kids will love the discovery tour, where the secrets of making the waxworks are revealed, while parents will wonder why some of the wax figures look 'Thunderbirds' in appearance.
☎ 01 47 70 85 05 🖥 www.grevin.com ✉ passage Jouffroy, 10-12 blvd Montmartre, 9e € €16/13.80/9 ⏲ 10am-7pm Ⓜ Grands-Boulevards ♿ limited ♨

PARIS FOR CHILDREN

Look for the icon (☺) listed with individual reviews in the Eating, Entertainment and Sleeping chapters for more kid-friendly options.

Children's Gallery – Centre Pompidou (5, D1)

The exhibitions give a wonderful entry to modern art, while the innovative workshops allow six to 12-year-olds a chance to get their hands dirty learning about modern art, architecture and performance.

☎ 01 44 78 49 13
🖳 www.centrepom pidou.fr ✉ Centre Pompidou, place Georges Pompidou, 4e € €8 ☼ workshops Wed & Sat afternoon; exhibition 1-7pm Wed-Mon Ⓜ Rambuteau ♿ limited ☺

Jardin d'Acclimatation (2, B2)

This amusement park is a Parisian favourite, with enough diverse attractions to the satisfy the most capricious youngsters. Horse rides, minigolf and a zoo are just some of the many attractions. For tech-heads there's the Explor@dome devoted to science and the media.

☎ 01 40 67 90 82
✉ Bois de Boulogne, 16e € €2.50/1.25 (under 4s free) ☼ 10am-6pm Oct-May, to 7pm Jun-Sep Ⓜ Les Sablons ♿ limited ☺

Musée de la Curiosité et de la Magie (5, E3)

The Museum of Curiosity and Magic in the 16th-century *caves* (cellars) of the house of the Marquis de Sade examines the ancient arts of magic, optical illusion and sleight of hand. It's great for curious kids, who'll love the magic shows (last one at 6pm) included in the price.

☎ 01 42 72 13 26
🖳 www.museedelama gie.com in French ✉ 11 rue St-Paul, 4e € €7/5 Ⓜ St-Paul ☼ 2-7pm Wed, Sat & Sun ☺

JEAN-BERNARD CARILLET

Try acclimatising to this attraction at Jardin d'Acclimatation

Musée de la Curiosité et de la Magie – don't be tricked (p39)

JEAN-BERNARD CARILLET

Palais de la Découverte
(3, C2) The excellent Palace of Discovery has many interactive science exhibits that make chemistry and physics appear to be fun subjects. The planetarium shows are great and on weekends and school holidays there are programmes involving intriguing live experiments for the kids to watch.
☎ 01 56 43 20 21
🖳 www.palais
-decouverte.fr in French
✉ av Franklin D Roosevelt, 8e € €6.50/4; planetarium €10/7.50
🕑 9.30am-6pm Tue-Sat, 10am-7pm Sun; planetarium 11.30am, 2.15, 3.30 & 4.45pm Ⓜ Champs Élysées Clemenceau
♿ limited ⛲

Parc Astérix (1, E1) This alternative to Disneyland Resort Paris (p46) has established ancient 'regions' for children to navigate their way around. Village of the Gauls, Roman Empire and Ancient Greece await, along with some frightening rides such as the wooden *Tonnerre de Zeus* and *Goudurix*. There

are six restaurants as well as 40 fast-food outlets. For a longer visit, there is also a hotel.
☎ 03 44 62 34 34
🖳 www.parcasterix.fr
✉ 36km from Paris, near Roissy airport
€ €32/23 🕑 10am-6pm Mon-Fri, 9.30am-7pm Sat & Sun & mid-Jul-Aug 🚆 RER line B3 from Châtelet or Gare du Nord to Roissy CDG 1, then shuttle bus (every 30mins 9am-2pm)
♿ limited ⛲

Parc Zoologique de Paris
(2, J5) Paris' main zoo accommodates over 1000 captives, which includes all of the usual exotic suspects. The zoo was inaugurated in 1931 and most of the animals are presented 'in the wild'. Well, as far as it can be realistically managed in a zoo situated right in a city.
☎ 01 44 75 20 10
🖳 www.mnhn.fr
✉ 53 av de St-Maurice, 12e € €8/5/free
🕑 9am-6pm Ⓜ Porte Dorée ♿ ⛲

Babysitting
L'Officiel des Spectacles, which is the weekly entertainment magazine that appears on newsstands every Wednesday, lists *gardes d'enfants* (babysitters) available in Paris.

- **Aprés la Classe** (3, G3; ☎ 01 42 33 75 45; 63 blvd Sébastopol, 1er; from €6 per hr, plus €10 subscription fee; Ⓜ Châtelet les Halles)
- **Baby Sitting Services** (☎ 01 46 21 33 16; from €6.30 per hr plus €10.90 subscription fee).
- **Étudiants de l'Institut Catholique** (3, E5; ☎ 01 44 39 60 24; 21; rue d'Assas, 6e; from €6 per hr plus €1.60 for each session; Ⓜ Rennes)

Out & About

WALKING TOURS
Highlight Hop

This walk takes in many of Paris' highlights in the one hit. Start at Paris' *point zéro* – the spot where all French metropolitan distances are measured from – the bronze star in **place du Parvis Notre Dame** (**1**, p9). After admiring Notre Dame, follow Quai aux Fleurs through the flower markets to the medieval **Conciergerie** (**2**, p32). Pass the Palais de Justice and the stunning **Ste-Chapelle** (**3**, p14) and take Quai des Orfèvres around to **square du Vert Galant** (**4**), for one of the best Seine views in Paris.

Cross **Pont Neuf** (**5**) and head through the Cour Carrée of the **Musée du Louvre** (**6**, p11) assessing the glass pyramid's appeal, while people-watching at **Café Marly** (**7**, p68). Pass under the **Arc de Triomphe du Carrousel** (**8**) to reach the elegant **Jardin des Tuileries** (**9**, p37).

Wander through the gardens to emerge at **place de la Concorde** (**10**, p35) with its striking fountains. Continue walking and you'll be on the **av des Champs Élysées** (**11**) heading towards the **Arc de Triomphe** (**12**, p10). Once you have delighted in the view here, embark on some shopping or finish the walk with a flourish by heading down to the **Eiffel Tower** (**13**, p8).

Heavy metal fan

JEAN-BERNARD CARILLET

---

distance 7km **duration** 3-4hr
▶ **start** Ⓜ Cité
⦿ **end** Ⓜ Charles de Gaulle-Étoile

Marvellous Marais Ramble

From the historic **Hôtel de Ville** (**1**, p32), turn left into café-lined rue des Archives. Turn right at the **Archives Nationales** (**2**), left past the **Hôtel de Rohan** (**3**) and right until you reach place de Thorigny and the **Musée Picasso** (**4**, p24).

Turn left into rue des Francs Bourgeois, passing the enchanting *hôtels particuliers* (private mansions) of **Musée Carnavalet** (**5**, p27), to reach elegant **place des Vosges** (**6**, p17). You can wander through **Maison de Victor Hugo** (**7**) at No 6; it is now a museum. A door in the southwest corner leads through the **Hôtel de Sully** (**8**, p32) and then on to bustling rue St-Antoine. Turn right, and after a detour to **place du Marché Ste-Catherine** (**9**), turn right again into rue Pavée for the **Guimard Synagogue** (**10**). Turn left into rue des Rosiers, the heart of the Jewish quarter and enjoy a falafel at **Chez Marianne** (**11**, p70).

Left into rue Vieille du Temple takes you across rue de Rivoli. Spicy rue François Miron, rue de Jouy and rue de l'Ave Maria lead to the **Hôtel de Sens** (**12**). Learn a trick or two at the **Musée de la Curiosité et de la Magie** (**13**, p39), or browse antiques in Village St-Paul (p56).

Slippin' 'n' slidin' past Hôtel de Ville

JEAN-BERNARD CARILLET

distance 3.5km **duration** 2½hr
▶ **start** Ⓜ Hôtel de Ville
● **end** Ⓜ St-Paul

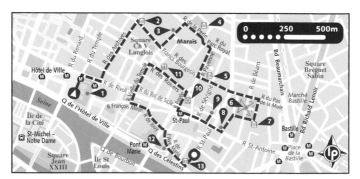

Left Bank Loop

From **Fontaine St-Michel** (**1**) cross blvd St-Michel and meander down to **Église St-Séverin** (**2**, p34). Cross to Église St-Julien-le-Pauvre and **square Viviani** (**3**), or browse books at **Shakespeare and Company** (**4**, p57).

Follow the *quais*, turning right at the **Institut du Monde Arabe** (**5**, p32). Turn left into rue Jussieu, then right into rue Linné, where you reach the **Roman Arènes de Lutèce** (**6**), a 2nd-century amphitheatre. Stroll the **Jardin des Plantes** (**7**, p36) or take tea at the **Mosquée de Paris** (**8**, p34).

Rue Daubenton heads towards the atmospheric markets, food shops and eateries on **rue Mouffetard** (**9**). Tale note of George Orwell's former digs at **6 rue Pot-de-Fer** (**10**), check out pretty **place de la Contrescarpe** (**11**) and **Hemingway's former residence** at 74 rue du Cardinal Lemoine (**12**). Continue along rue Descartes, then turn left into rue Clovis for **Église St-Étienne du Mont** (**13**, p34) as well as the **Panthéon** (**14**, p33).

Follow rue Soufflot, with the **Sorbonne** (**15**) on your right, to the **Jardin du Luxembourg** (**16**, p21). Cobbled rue Servandoni leads to the enormous **Église St-Sulpice** (**17**, p34) and shopping around **place du Quebec** (**18**). Cross blvd St-Germain to the **Église St-Germain des Prés** (**19**, p34), and imbibe at **Café de Flore** (**20**, p83) to your left, before taking bustling rue de Buci and rue St-André des Arts back to place St-Michel.

Feast your senses along rue Mouffetard

distance 6km **duration** 3hr
▶ **start** Ⓜ St Michel
◉ **end** Ⓜ St-Michel

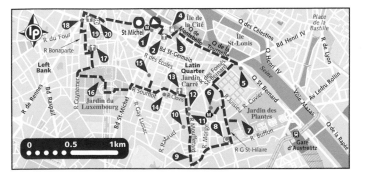

Montmartre Memories

Starting on shop-lined rue Lepic, to your left is the saucy **Moulin Rouge** (**1**, p92) and to your right is the 'educational' **Musée de l'Érotisme** (**2**, p38). Stay on rue Lepic, passing **Van Gogh's home** (3rd floor, No 54) (**3**). After rue Lepic curves right you'll spot the two evocative **windmills** (Moulin de la Gallette, **4**) & (Moulin Radet, **5**). Turn left into rue Girardon and descend the stairs from place Dalida into rue St-Vincent, passing the **Cimetière St-Vincent** (**6**). Before you turn right past Paris' only innercity **vineyard** (Le Close de Montmartre, **7**) on your left is bohemian **Au Lapin Agile** (**8**, p89). Turn left into rue Cortot, passing **Montmartre's oldest house** (**9**) at No 12–14, now a museum, and **Eric Satie's house** (**10**) at No 6 rue Cortot.

Turn right at the **water tower** (**11**) and then left to reach **Sacré Cœur** (**12**, p16) for stunning Paris vistas. Walk past ancient **St-Pierre de Montmartre** (**13**) to experience the portraitists at work in **place du Tertre** (**14**).

Follow rue Poulbot past the **Espace Montmartre Salvador Dalí** (**15**, p30) at No 11. Use the steps from **place du Calvaire** (**16**) into rue Gabrielle, turning right to reach **place Émile Goudeau** (**17**), descend the steps turning left at rue des Abbesses towards the Guimard-designed metro entrance at **place des Abbesses** (**18**, p35).

JEAN-BERNARD CARILLET

Hold your hemlines, it's Moulin Rouge!

distance 2.5km **duration** 2hr
▶ **start** Ⓜ Blanche
◉ **end** Ⓜ Abbesses

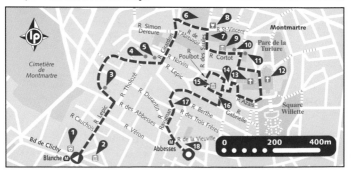

DAY TRIPS
Château de Fontainebleau (1, E3)

While Château de Versailles (p20) is such a drawcard, the much more relaxed atmosphere at this elegant Renaissance chateau coupled with the beauty of the adjacent forest – where royalty went hunting for centuries – make this well worth visiting. A popular royal chateau from François 1 (1494–1547) onwards, it is one of the most richly decorated and furnished chateaux in France, with every centimetre of wall and ceiling space adorned with wood panelling, gilded carvings, frescoes, tapestries and paintings.

In addition to the magnificent apartments, and courtyards, the **Musée Napoléon 1er** has personal effects belonging to Napoleon (to access the museum, inquire at the ticket counter), and there are several beautiful gardens as well as the forest to wander through.

> **Information**
> *65km southeast of Paris*
> - 🚉 Gare de Lyon to Fontainebleau-Avon (35-60min)
> - ☎ 01 60 71 50 70
> - 🖳 www.musee-chateau-fontaine bleau.fr in French
> - € €5.50/4
> - 🕙 9.30am-6pm Wed-Mon Jun-Sep, to 5pm Wed-Mon Oct-May
> - ✖ Chez Arrighi (☎ 01 64 22 29 43; 53 rue de France)

Cathédrale Notre Dame de Chartres (1, C3)

The magnificent 13th-century Notre Dame de Chartres, dominating the medieval town from which it rises, is one of the crowning architectural accomplishments of Western civilisation. The cathedral's astonishing original stained-glass windows (renowned for their intensely blue tones), which incorporate astrological symbols, ornamented portals and two soaring spires – one Gothic style and the other Romanesque – make it a compelling day trip outside Paris.

The cathedral's collection of holy relics – particularly the Sainte Chemise, alleged to have been worn by the Virgin Mary when she gave birth to Jesus – was a major attraction for pilgrims during the Middle Ages.

The adjacent **Musée des Beaux-Arts** (Fine Arts Museum; ☎ 02 37 36 41 39, 29; Cloître Notre-Dame) has some outstanding pieces from the 16th to 19th centuries in its collection.

> **Information**
> *90km southwest of Paris*
> - 🚉 SNCF train from Gare Montparnasse to Chartres (45-60min)
> - ☎ 02 37 21 22 07
> - 🖳 www.cathedrale-chartres.com in French
> - € *Clocher Neuf* (New Bell Tower) €4.60/3.10; crypt tours €2.60/2; museum €2.45/1.20
> - 🕙 cathedral 8.30am-7.30pm, 10am-noon & 2-6pm Mon & Wed-Sat, 2-6pm Sun May-Oct, to 5pm Mon & Wed-Sat, to 5pm Sun Nov-Apr
> - ℹ tourist office (☎ 02 37 18 26 26, place de la Cathédrale)
> - ✖ Café Serpente (opposite cathedral)

Disneyland Resort Paris (1, F2)

While the theme park formerly known as 'Eurodisney' has been on a financial roller-coaster ride scarier than its *Indiana Jones and the Temple of Peril* attraction, it is still the most popular fee-paying attraction in Europe. Disneyland Resort Paris (which it is now called) has three main entertainment areas: the **Disney Village**, including hotels, shops, restaurants and clubs; **Disneyland Park** with its five theme parks; and the less frequented **Walt Disney Studios**, which brings film, animation and TV production to life. The RER and TGV train stations separate the first two locations, and Walt Disney Studios is situated next to Disneyland Park.

Information
32km east of Paris
- 🚈 RER line A4 to Marne-la-Vallée-Chessy (35-40min)
- ☎ 01 60 30 60 30
- 🖥 www.disneylandparis.com
- € Disneyland Park *or* Walt Disney Studios Park day pass adult/child 3-11 €40/30 Apr-Oct, €39/29 Nov-Mar; Walt Disney Studios Park entry gives you free entry after 5pm to Disneyland Park
- 🕙 Disneyland Park 9am-8pm daily (check website for variations)
- 🍴 More than 50 restaurants

Musée Claude Monet – Giverny (1, C1)

Fans of Monet's *Water Lilies* paintings won't want to miss visiting the tiny village of Giverny, where the impressionist lived from 1883 to his death in 1926. While an unfortunately placed road has spoilt the atmosphere of Monet's estate, his famous pastel pink-and-green house, Water Lily studio and seasonal flower-filled gardens are still intact.

A tunnel leads under the road to the Jardin d'Eau (Water Garden), where Monet dug a pool, planted water lilies and constructed the famous Japanese bridge, which has since been rebuilt. Draped with purple wisteria, the bridge blends into the asymmetrical foreground and background, creating the intimate atmosphere for which the 'Painter of Light' was famous.

Not far from here is the **Musée d'Art Américain** (☎ 02 32 51 94 65; €5.50/4/3) containing the works of many American Impressionists such as Theodore Robinson and Lilla Cabot Perry.

Information
76km west of Paris
- 🚈 Gare St-Lazare to Vernon (45min), then Val de Seine bus (7km)
- ☎ 02 32 51 28 21
- 🖥 www.fondation-monet.com
- € €5.50/4/3
- 🕙 9.30am-6pm Tue-Sun Apr-Oct
- 🍴 Auberge du Vieux Moulin (☎ 02 32 51 46 15; 21 rue de la Falaise)

Monet's garden leaves a strong impression

ORGANISED TOURS

Bicycle Tours

**Fat Tire Bike Tours
(3, B5)** This English-speaking company (formerly Mike's Bike Tours) offers half-day tours of the city, as well four- to five-hour night tours – perfect for a hot summer night. They also do a Versailles tour and a Monet tour. See right for the Segway tour.
☎ 01 56 58 10 54
🖳 www.fattirebike toursparis.com ✉ 24 rue Edgar Faure, 15e
€ €24/22 half-day
🕑 11am Mar-Apr & Sep-Nov, 11am & 3.30pm May-Aug Ⓜ La Motte-Picquet Grenelle

**Paris à Vélo c'est Sympa
(5, F1)** This longstanding company offers a range of interesting half-day thematic bike tours (English spoken) covering central and outer Paris, as well as dawn, night and full-day (July to August) excursions.
☎ 01 48 87 60 01
🖳 www.parisvelosympa .com ✉ 22 rue Alphonse Baudin, 11e € €30/26, deposit €250 per bike or passport 🕑 9.30am-1pm & 2-6.30pm Mon-Fri, 9am-7pm Sat & Sun Apr-Oct Ⓜ Richard Lenoir

Boat Tours

Bateaux Parisiens (3, A3)
One-hour Seine cruises with commentary in multiple languages. They offer lunch and dinner cruises as well.
☎ 01 44 11 33 55
🖳 www.bateauxparis iens.com ✉ Port de la Bourdonnais, 7e

A Seine-ible way to view Paris is by boat

JEAN-BERNARD CARILLET

€ €9.50/4.50 🕑 ½ hourly 10am-11pm Apr-Oct, hourly 10am-1pm & 5-8pm, ½ hourly, 1-5pm & 8-10pm Nov-Mar Ⓜ Pont de l'Alma

Canal Croisières (3, E3)
Three-hour cruise along the Seine and canals from the Musée d'Orsay to Parc de la Villette. Booking required.
☎ 01 42 40 96 97
✉ Quai Anatole France (3, E3) or Parc de la Villette (2, H1) € €16/12/9 🕑 depart Musée d'Orsay (3, E3) 9.30am & return Parc de la Villette 2.30pm late Mar–mid-Nov, also

departs 2.35pm & 6.15pm Jul-Aug

Canauxrama (2, G2)
Three-hour cruises along charming Canal St-Martin and Canal de l'Ourcq between Port de l'Arsenal and Parc de la Villette.
☎ 01 42 39 15 00
🖳 www.canauxrama .com ✉ Port de l'Arsenal, opp 50 blvd de la Bastille, 12e; Bassin de la Villette, 13 Quai de la Loire, 19e
€ €13/11/8 Mon-Fri, €13 after noon Sat & Sun 🕑 from Port de l'Arsenal & Parc de la Villette 9.45am & 2.30pm, Mar-Nov

Segue to a Segway

There's nothing quite like a tour of Paris on a Segway® Human Transporter (HT). This two-wheeled personal transportation device is still a rare sight on city streets so take your chance to test-drive one and see Paris at the same time. There's 30 minutes of instruction before the tour begins and riding one becomes second nature very quickly, which is odd considering there's no accelerator or brakes. The tours are either day or night and last four to five hours (€70). Tours are run by Fat Tire Bike Tours (left).

Compagnie de Bateaux Mouches (3, C3) Bateaux Mouches runs the biggest tour boats on the Seine. Cruises depart from Pont de l'Alma, and pass the Statue of Liberty and Eiffel Tower in the west, and Île St-Louis in the east; cruises last one hour. They also have lunch and dinner cruises.
☎ 01 42 25 96 10 🖥 www.bateaux mouches.com ✉ Pont de l'Alma, 8e Ⓜ Alma Marceau 🕙 every ½hr 10am-8pm, every 20 min 8-11pm mid-Mar–mid-Nov € €7/4

Bus Tours
Cityrama (3, E3) This company runs 2-hour city tours (multilanguage taped commentary) and night city tours in high-tech buses with panoramic windows, and also offers excursions further afield, such as Chartres and Versailles.
☎ 01 44 55 61 00 🖥 www.cityrama.com ✉ meet at 4 place des

Pyramides Ⓜ Palais Royal 🕙 tours 11am, noon, 2pm & 3pm Apr-Oct, 10am & 2pm Nov-Mar € €24

Paris l'Open Tour (3, E1) L'Open Tour operates open-deck buses that run along four circuits (central Paris, 2¼ hours; Montmartre–Grands Boulevards, 1¼ hours; Bastille–Bercy, one hour; and Montparnasse–St-Germain, one hour) daily year-round. You can jump on and off at over 50 bus stops and there's commentary in English and French.
☎ 01 42 66 56 56 🖥 www.paris-opentour .com ✉ 13 rue Auber, 9e € €25/12, 2-day pass €28/12 🕙 9.30am-6.30pm, to 8pm Apr-Oct Ⓜ Havre Caumartin

Other Tours
Paris Hélicoptère (1, E2) With its base at the Aéroport du Bourget, north of Paris, this company provides 80km circular

flights over Paris every Sunday, which last for 25 minutes. Book 10 days in advance. You can reach Le Bourget by RER line B or by RATP bus No 350 from Gare du Nord, Gare de l'Est or Porte de la Chapelle, or bus No 152 from Porte de la Villette (stop: Musée de l'Air et de l'Espace).
☎ 01 48 35 90 44 🖥 www.paris-helicop tere.com ✉ Aéroport du Bourget € 122 🕙 9am-6pm Sun

Walking Tours
Paris Walking Tours This long-established, small English-speaking team provide two-hour daily walks through Paris, including Montmartre, the Marais, the Latin Quarter as well as the Paris of Hemingway and inevitably, a *Da Vinci Code* walk. Meeting points advised on reservation.
☎ 01 48 09 21 40 🖥 www.paris-walks.com € €10/7/5

Greet Parisian architecture face-to-face on a bus tour

JEAN-BERNARD CARILLET

Shopping

From his apartment overlooking the charming place des Vosges, Victor Hugo wrote in *Les Misérables*, 'All that can be found anywhere can be found in Paris'. That is still the case in his old neighbourhood alone where the Marais' cobblestone streets are lined with shops selling ethnic jewellery, oriental interiors, world music, Mexican photography and African art, alongside the chic Parisian boutiques, bookshops and gourmet food stores. One of the delights of shopping in Paris is that it reflects the ethnic mix of the population – and you'll find anything you desire. Unlike many cities, Paris doesn't have a shopping 'centre', rather there are many *quartiers* (quarters), such as the Bastille, St-Germain, St-Paul and Canal St-Martin offering an array of speciality shops.

Think big – it's the av des Champs Élysées

Most shops open from 10am to 7pm, five days a week, including Saturday, but they may open earlier, close later, shut for lunch, or open in the afternoon on Monday or Tuesday. Many shops have a late opening hours *(nocturnes)* one night a week. Small shops often shut in August, and only shops in tourist areas like the av des Champs Élysées and the Marais open on Sunday.

Credit cards can be used everywhere. Although Parisians often use personal cheques, travellers cheques are rarely accepted (especially in boutique shops). If you're not an EU resident, you can get a TVA (sales tax) refund of up to 17% if you spend more than €182 in any one shop. Show your passport and fill out a *détaxe* (duty-free sales) form in the shop. At least three hours before departing, take the form and your purchases to the customs desk at the point where you leave the EU. The refund is usually credited to your credit card or mailed by cheque within three months.

CLOTHING & SHOE SIZES

Women's Clothing

Aust/UK	8	10	12	14	16	18
Europe	36	38	40	42	44	46
Japan	5	7	9	11	13	15
USA	6	8	10	12	14	16

Women's Shoes

Aust/USA	5	6	7	8	9	10
Europe	35	36	37	38	39	40
France only	35	36	38	39	40	42
Japan	22	23	24	25	26	27
UK	3½	4½	5½	6½	7½	8½

Men's Clothing

Aust	92	96	100	104	108	112
Europe	46	48	50	52	54	56

Japan	S	M	M		L	
UK/USA	35	36	37	38	39	40

Men's Shirts (Collar Sizes)

Aust/Japan	38	39	40	41	42	43
Europe	38	39	40	41	42	43
UK/USA	15	15½	16	16½	17	17½

Men's Shoes

Aust/UK	7	8	9	10	11	12
Europe	41	42	43	44½	46	47
Japan	26	27	27.5	28	29	30
USA	7½	8½	9½	10½	11½	12½

Measurements approximate only;
try before you buy.

DEPARTMENT STORES

BHV (5, D2) Shoppers flock to Bazar de l'Hôtel de Ville for the huge range of hardware in what is otherwise a fairly straightforward department store.
☎ 01 42 74 90 00
✉ 2-64 rue de Rivoli, 4e
🕑 9.30am-7pm Mon-Sat (to 9pm Wed, to 8pm Sat)
Ⓜ Hôtel de Ville

Forum des Halles (5, C1) The best thing about this crowded underground shopping mall is the expansive FNAC department store, especially its excellent digital media and photography section. You'll also find clothes, shoes, accessories, food, cinemas and a swimming pool.
☎ 01 44 76 96 56
✉ rues Berger & Rambuteau, 1er
🕑 10am-7.30pm Mon-Sat Ⓜ Les Halles

Galeries Lafayette (3, E1) Shopping under the magnificent glass dome should be reason enough to visit, but tens of thousands of brand-name items, dozens of individual designers boutiques, and a champagne bar, also make this shopping experience a must.
☎ 01 42 82 34 56
🖥 www.galeriesla fayette.com ✉ 40 blvd Haussmann, 9e
🕑 9.30am-7pm Mon-Sat (to 9pm Thu) Ⓜ Auber

La Samaritaine (5, B1) Highlights at this *belle époque* (early 20th-century; literally 'beautiful age') gem are the jaw-dropping views across the Seine from the restaurant and rooftop terraces and its super-stylish Kenzo store designed by film-set designer Emmanuelle Duplay.
☎ 01 40 41 20 20 ✉ 19 rue de la Monnaie, 1er
🕑 9.30am-7pm Mon-Wed & Fri, to 10pm Thu, to 8pm Sat) Ⓜ Pont Neuf

Le Bon Marché (3, E5) Gustave Eiffel built Paris' first department store,

Hot Shopping Spots
Bercy Village, 12e (2, G5; Palais Omnisports de Paris-Bercy) Interior design, homewares, boutiques.
Canal St-Martin, 10e (3, H1) Boho fashion, art and design bookshops.
Latin Quarter, 5e (5, B4) Books, stationery, quirky gift shops.
Marais, 3e (5, E2) Hip fashion, jewellery, interior designers, quirky speciality shops.
Opéra, 9e (3, E2) Major department stores, clothing, perfume, cosmetics.
Place de la Madeleine, 8e (3, D2) Gourmet food shops, chocolate shops, tea rooms.
Place des Abbesses & rue des Martyrs, 18e (4, C2) Young designers, retro clothing, music.
Place Vendôme, 1er (3, E2) Designer fashion, jewellery, luxury goods.
Rue de Rivoli & Les Halles, 1er & 2e (5, B2) Clothes, cosmetics, books, souvenirs.
Rue Étienne Marcel, 2e (3, G3) Urban streetwear, club gear, record shops.
Rue Keller, Sedaine & Charonne, 11e (2, G4) Grungy boutiques, record shops.
St-Germain, 6e (5, B3) Art, antiques, designer clothes, shoes, accessories.
St-Paul, 4e (5, E2) Antiques, interior design, books.
Sentier, 2e (3, G2) Clothes, jewellery, kitchenware.
Triangle d'Or & rue du Faubourg St-Honoré, 8e & 1er (3, B2) *Haute couture*, jewellery, art.
Viaduc des Arts, 12e (2, H5) Ateliers, galleries, interior design shops.

and perhaps its most stylish following a recent renovation by Andrée Putman. Highlights include the glorious **La Grande Épicerie de Paris** (🖳 www.lagrande epicerie.fr) with its enormous range of global gourmet delicacies (perfect for preparing for a picnic) as well as Sébastien Gaudard's chic Delicabar. Try resisting the sweet snacks such as chocolate fondue and his signature bubble cakes.

☎ 01 44 39 80 00
🖳 www.lebonmarche
.fr ✉ 22 rue de Sèvres, 7e ⏲ 9.30am-7pm Mon-Wed, Fri, 10am-9pm Thu, 9.30am-8pm Sat
Ⓜ Sèvres Babylone

Poodling products galore at Le Bon Marché

Le Printemps (3, E1)
Famous for its gorgeous Art Nouveau cupola, the most expansive of Parisian department store's four buildings holds the world's largest beauty department, endless floors of fashion, including cutting-edge designers. The Citadium emporium stocks an enormous range of sports gear especially cool surf, skate and snow stuff.

☎ 01 42 82 50 00
🖳 www.printemps.com
✉ 64 blvd Haussmann, 9e ⏲ 9.35am-7pm Mon-Sat, to 10pm Thu
Ⓜ Havre Caumartin

FLEA MARKETS

Visiting the easily accessible *marchés aux puces* (flea markets) of Paris is on the to-do list if you love browsing for unexpected treasures among the bric-a-brac and *brocante* (second-hand goods). Bargaining is expected!

Marché aux Puces d'Aligre (2, G4) The most central and smallest of Paris' flea markets is a good place to rummage for old clothes and accessories, books and bric-a-brac. Adjoining it is a great fresh produce market and gourmet shops in the nearby streets.
✉ place d'Aligre, 12e ⏲ early-1pm Tue-Sun Ⓜ Ledru Rollin

Marché aux Puces de Montreuil (2, J4)
This popular market, established in the 19th century, boasts 500 stalls selling second-hand clothes, old jewellery, furniture, crockery and car parts!
✉ av de la Porte de Montreuil, 20e ⏲ 7am-7pm Sat-Mon Ⓜ Porte de Montreuil

Marché aux Puces de St-Ouen (2, F1)
Also dating back to the 19th century, this vast flea market is said to be Europe's largest with 2000-plus stalls grouped into 10 marches, each with their own specialities – everything from Art Deco collectables to retro clothing – and their own pickpockets.

✉ rue des Rosiers, av Michelet, rue Voltaire, rue Paul Bert & rue Jean-Henri Fabre, 18e ⏲ 7.30am-7pm Sat-Mon Ⓜ Porte de Clignancourt

Marché aux Puces de la Porte de Vanves (2, D6)
This market is the place to come for collectors of perfume bottles, old dolls and children's toys, faded photographs and postcards, costume jewellery and other curios.
✉ av Georges Lafenestre & av Marc Sangnier, 14e ⏲ 7am-6pm Sat & Sun Ⓜ Porte de Vanves

FASHION

Abou d'Abi Bazar (5, E2)
Widely written about, this hip Marais store lives up to its reputation for stocking stylish, affordable and ever-changing collections by cool young designers such as Vanessa Bruno, Paul & Joe, Tara Jarmon and Stella Forest.
☎ 01 42 77 96 98 ✉ 10 rue des Francs-Bourgeois, 3e ⏱ 10.30am-7pm Tue-Sat, 2-7pm Sun-Mon Ⓜ St-Paul

Antoine et Lili (4, D3)
These colourful kooky boutiques sell silky Chinese pyjamas, adjustable wraparound hippy skirts, trousers and bohemian knits. Also, motivated by the owners' desire to display all the things from around the world that excite them, ethnic jewellery and accessories, sparkling Indian bindis, Japanese slippers, woolly Peruvian hats, Mexican tequila trays, kitsch postcards, scented candles and incense.
☎ 01 42 58 10 22 💻 www.antoineetlili .com ✉ 90 rue des Martyrs, 18e ⏱ 10am-7.30pm Mon-Sat Ⓜ Abbesses

Beyouk (3, J4) Funky, comfy colourful clothes designed with the global traveller in mind – their hip marketing shows young women wearing their gear as they head for places like Helsinki, Kyoto or St Petersburg.
☎ 01 40 21 02 20 ✉ 7-9 rue de Charonne, 11e

Preparing a plan of attack outside Antoine et Lili

⏱ 11am-7pm Tue-Sat, 2-7pm Sun Ⓜ Ledru Rollin

Didier Ludot (3, F3)
These fabulous stores are crammed with vintage *haute couture* creations – little black dresses from Dior, evening gowns from Givenchy, the famous Balenciaga coats, sharp Chanel suits, Hermès bags and accessories – all coveted collector's items.
☎ 01 42 96 06 56 ✉ 19-24 Galerie de Montpensier, 1er ⏱ 10.30am-7pm Mon-Sat Ⓜ Palais Royal

Heaven (4, C3) This young designer's his-and-her collections have a decidedly retro feel to them – long velvet coat dresses, brocade jackets, textured woollen suits, feathered brooches, corduroy jackets and vinyl handbags.
☎ 01 44 92 92 92 ✉ 83 rue des Martyrs, 18e ⏱ 11am-7.30pm

Tue-Sat, 2pm-7.30pm Sun Ⓜ Abbesses

Kiliwatch (3, G3) A huge range of cool and colourful street and clubwear, quality second-hand clothes, sneakers, bags and accessories, plus graphic design and photography books, magazines, and CDs. Always packed full of hipsters checking out the scene.
☎ 01 42 21 17 37 ✉ 64 rue Tiquetonne, 2e ⏱ 2-7pm Mon, 11am-7pm Tue-Sat Ⓜ Étienne Marcel

Madelios (3, E2) This one-stop men's designer department store stocks an expansive selection of classic and contemporary suits, casual wear, shoes and accessories, plus there's a hairdressing/beauty salon, café and exhibition space.
☎ 01 53 45 00 00 ✉ 23 blvd de la Madeleine, 8e ⏱ 10am-7pm Mon-Sat Ⓜ Madeleine

Nuits de Satin (3, J3)
This fabulous store sells only the best quality vintage and retro lingerie, swimwear, couture and accessories, specialising in the period from 1900 to 1950.
☎ 01 43 57 65 05 ✉ 9 rue Oberkampf, 11e
🕒 12.30pm-7.30pm Mon-Sat Ⓜ Filles du Cavaliere

Onze (3, J3) Refined tailoring, defined structure, textured fabrics and idiosyncratic details unite the diverse collections of French and Japanese labels, such as Just In Case and Takashi Yokoyama, at this light, airy store.
☎ 01 43 55 32 11 ✉ 11 rue Oberkampf, 11e
🕒 Mon-Sat 11am-7pm Ⓜ Filles des Cavaliers

Patricia Louisor (4, C3)
Wrap yourself in the 'cheap and chic' collections of young designer, Patricia Louisor, whose latest collection includes bright basics such as long loosely tied linen coats, high-wasted flares, low-cut

---

Paris Designers: Bonnes Addresses
For serious fashionistas, try:
agnès b (3, G3; rue du Jour, 1er)
Barbara Bui (3, C2; 50 av Montaigne, 8e)
Chanel (3, C2; 40-42 av Montaigne, 8e)
Christian Dior (3, C2; 30 av Montaigne, 8e)
Commes des Garçons (3, D2; 54 rue du Faubourg St-Honoré, 8e)
Givenchy (3, B3; 8 av Georges V, 8e)
Hermès (3, D2; 24 rue du Faubourg St-Honoré, 8e)
Inès de la Fressange (3, B2; 14 av Montaigne, 8e)
Issey Miyake (5, E2; 3 place des Vosges, 4e)
Jean-Paul Gaultier (3, F2; 6 rue Vivienne, 2e)
Lolita Lempicka (3, B2; 78 av Marceau, 8e)
Louis Vuitton (3, B2; 101 av des Champs Élysées, 8e)
Martine Sitbon (3, E4; 13 rue de Grenelle, 7e)
Sonia Rykiel (5, A2; 175 blvd St-Germain, 6e)
Thierry Mugler (3, C2; 49 av Montaigne, 8e)
Yves Saint Laurent (3, D2; 38 rue du Faubourg St-Honoré)

---

flowing skirts, and colourful knits.
☎ 01 42 62 10 42
✉ 16 rue Houdon, 18e
🕒 12-8pm Mon-Sun
Ⓜ Abbesses

Tatiana Lebedev (5, E1)
This Moscow émigré's most recent FuturWare Lab collection presented tailored black, slate,

grey and chocolate skirts and jackets, punctuated by dazzling colour, asymmetrical cutting and obtrusive stitching, textured fabrics and leather.
☎ 01 42 77 80 89 ✉ 64 rue Vieille du Temple, 1er 🕒 11am-2pm & 2.30-7pm Tue-Sat
Ⓜ Rambuteau

JEAN-BERNARD CARILLET

Hipsters show their stripes at Kiliwatch

JEWELLERY & ACCESSORIES

Colette (3, E2) Proclaiming to specialise in style, Colette stocks a selection of cool stuff not sold elsewhere in Paris: stylish sneakers, accessories, jewellery and watches, high-tech gadgets (including custom coloured iPods), cool CDs, design books and magazines. There's beauty products by Nars and Remède, and clothes by Comme des Garçons, Marni, Pucci and Alexander McQueen.
☎ 01 55 35 33 90
🖥 www.colette.fr
✉ 213 rue St-Honoré, 1er 🕑 10.30am-7.30pm Mon-Sat Ⓜ Tuileries

Little black numbers with a twist at Colette

Emmanuelle Zysman (4, C3) Once in the purple shop you won't want to leave without purchasing a Zysman funky handbag, matching jewellery pieces and accessories. Her collections are seasonal and thematic, such as Japanese-inspired pieces featuring pink cherry blossoms and water lilies.

☎ 01 42 52 01 00
✉ 81 rue des Martyrs, 18e 🕑 10.30am-1pm & 3-7.30pm Tue-Sat Ⓜ Abbesses

Il pour l'Homme (3, E3) This hip store, in a renovated paint shop, shows off its super-stylish accessories for men in 19th-century display counters and chests of drawers – everything a man could want, from tie clips to cigar cutters.

☎ 01 42 60 43 56
✉ 209 rue St-Honoré, 1er 🕑 10am-7pm Mon-Sat Ⓜ Tuileries

Jamin Puech (3, G1) Making innovative use of rarely-used materials, Isabelle Puech and Benoît Jamin's handbags are considered by many to be works of art, but the shop alone is a worth a visit for its idiosyncratic styling.
☎ 01 40 22 08 32 ✉ 61 rue d'Hauteville, 10e 🕑 11am-7pm Mon & Sat, 10am-7pm Tue-Fri Ⓜ Poissonière

Metal Pointus (5, E3) You'll find it almost impossible to leave this store empty handed when confronted with such varied collections of super stylish and striking silver jewellery and accessories from young French designers.
☎ 01 40 29 44 34 ✉ 19 rue des Francs Bourgeois, 4e 🕑 11am-7pm Mon-Sat Ⓜ St-Paul

All that glints, glistens and drapes at Emmanuelle Zysman

BEAUTY & PERFUME

Detaille (3, F1) Countess de Presle opened this charming store in 1905 after suffering from dry skin from driving in her windshield-less car. She hired chemist Marcellin Berthelot to create a hydrating lotion, Baume Automobile, the first in a range of high-quality, classic beauty and perfume products, still sold in exquisite bottles and extremely elegant packaging.
☎ 01 48 78 68 50 ✉ 10 rue Saint-Lazare, 9e ⊙ 10.30am-7.30pm Mon-Sat

L'Artisan Parfumeur (5, D2) Sensual and unusual fragrances such as tea and gingerbread, rose and fig, come in classical bottles, while 'scented curiosities' such as aromatic 'dream-catchers' and colourful taffeta 'magic sticks' in an orange satin case delight with their whimsy.
☎ 01 48 04 55 66 ✉ 32 rue du Bourg Tibourg, 4e Ⓜ St-Paul ⊙ 10.30am-7pm Mon-Sat

L'Occitane en Provence (5, E2) Vanilla bath salts, magnolia soap, mimosa body milk, orange-blossom water, olive-oil hand cream, and other luxuriant beauty products can be found at this quintessentially French shop. A policy of no testing on animals and environmentally friendly packaging make it very popular.
☎ 01 42 77 96 67 ✉ 17 rue des Francs-Bourgeois

4e ⊙ 11am-7pm Mon, 10am-7pm Tue-Wed, 10am-8pm Thu-Sat Ⓜ St-Paul

Séphora (3, B2) The flagship of this beauty supermarket stocks over 12,000 fragrances and cosmetics, including more obscure products alongside the big-name brands, most of which are available for sampling. Branches throughout Paris.
☎ 01 53 93 22 50 ✉ 70 av des Champs Élysées, 8e ⊙ Mon-Sat 10am-1am, Sun noon-1am Ⓜ Franklin D Roosevelt

Live the Life of Le Flâneur

Some of the best specialist shopping in Paris is in the sublime *passages* – marble-floored, glass-roofed shopping corridors, streaming with natural light. These elegant forerunners to department stores and malls appeared in the 1820s. Walter Benjamin scrutinised the *passages* as he walked them from 1927 to 1940, documenting their significance in *The Arcades Project*. He reflects upon the intricacies of everyday life in 19th-century Paris, covering topics like cafés, collecting, commodity fetishism, fashion, window displays, advertising, architecture, the world exhibitions, photography, panoramas, prostitution and progress. Benjamin's focus is *flâneurie*, the activity of the *flâneur*, an aimless stroller compelled to explore the streets and scout the passages, getting to know his geography. If, like a *flâneur*, you're intoxicated by street life, a stroll through the following 'cities in miniature' is a must:

Galerie Vivienne (3, F2; 6 rue Vivienne to 4 rue des Petits Champs, 2e) Jewellery, wine store, designer fashion, children's toys and books.
Passage des Panoramas (3, F2; off rue Vivienne, 2e) Antiques, bric-a-brac, old postcards and stamps.
Passage du Grand Cerf (3, G3; 145 rue St-Denis to 10 rue Dussoubs, 2e) Contemporary jewellery, funky fashion, eccentric hats, stylish lighting.
Passage Jouffroy & Passage Verdeau (3, F1; 10-12 blvd Montmartre, 9e) Miniature dollhouse toys, movie memorabilia, antique cameras, old books, postcards and a cross-stitch specialist!
Galerie Véro Dodat (3, F3; 19 rue Jean-Jacques Rousseau to 2 rue du Bouloi, 1er) Bric-a-brac, antique dolls, curios.

JEAN-BERNARD CARILLET

A battalion of perfume bottles at Shiseido

Shiseido (3, F3) This seductive purple, mirrored salon in the Palais Royal arcades showcases Serge Luten's olfactory genius. Customised scents are displayed on pedestals like sculptures. It's worth a peek for its candied violets in dishes and pink orchids.
☎ 01 49 27 09 09
✉ 142 Galerie de Valois, 1er ☽ 9am-7pm Mon-Sat Ⓜ Louvre

ART, ANTIQUES & COLLECTABLES

You'll find an array of art galleries and shops dealing in antiques and collectables around av Matignon (8e), Beaubourg (3e), St-Germain (6e), Bastille (11e/12e), rue Louise Weiss (13e), Village St-Paul (4e), rue du Bac (7e) and rue du Faubourg St-Honoré (8e). Keep in mind that many close in August. Exhibitions are listed in *Pariscope* and *L'Officiel des Spectacles*.

Carré Rive Gauche (5, A1) Home to over 100 commercial galleries, ateliers and shops, the fascinating Left Bank Square (the narrow streets within quai Voltaire, rue l'Université, rue du Bac and rue des Saints Pères) is your one-stop shop for fine art, antiques, and old and modern collectables.
☎ 01 42 60 70 10
🖥 www.carrerive gauche.com ✉ quai Voltaire 7e ☽ 10am-6.00pm Mon-Sat
Ⓜ rue du Bac

Drouot (3, F2) If your French isn't ready for the rapid bids at Paris' most respected auction house, in business for about 150 years, you can bid online for that unique *objet d'art*. Auction details are onsite or in the *Gazette de L'Hôtel Drouot* available at newsstands.

☎ 01 48 00 20 20
🖥 www.gazette-drouot .com ✉ 9 rue Drouot, 9e ☽ sales 2-6pm; viewing 11am-6pm day prior to auction & 11am-noon sale day Ⓜ Richelieu Drouot

Le Louvre des Antiquaires (5, B1) Classical antiquities, expensive antique furniture, clocks, carpets, jewellery and fine art can be admired in the 250 shops scattered over three floors of this enormous building. Antique lovers could easily spend days here poking around.
☎ 01 42 97 27 00
🖥 www.louvre -antiquaires.com ✉ 2 place du Palais Royal, 1er ☽ 11am-7pm Tue-Sun
Ⓜ Palais Royal

L'Objet Qui Parle (4, D3) If your taste slants towards quirky collectables, such as

unusual patterned China or multicoloured crystal candelabra, you'll find what you're looking for at 'Objects That Speak'. On our last visit, however, a bust of Christ and some stuffed cows left us speechless.
☎ 06 09 67 05 30 ✉ 86 rue des Martyrs, 18e ☽ 1pm-7.30pm Tue-Sat
Ⓜ Abbesses

Virtuoses de la Reclame (5, E3) While the colourful window display of tin objects, including retro posters, cigarette boxes, ashtrays, kitchen tins, might beckon you inside, get those second-hand shop prices out of your mind. With or without rust, these are rare pieces and antique prices apply.
☎ 01 42 72 07 86 ✉ 5 rue Saint Paul, 4e ☽ 2-7pm Tue-Fri Ⓜ St-Paul

BOOKS

Album (5, C3) Comic books *(bandes dessinées)* are enormously popular in France and Album has the best selection, including Tintin, Japanese manga and erotic comics.
☎ 01 43 25 85 19
🖳 www.album.fr ✉ 84 Blvd St-Germain, 5e
🕙 10am-8pm Mon-Sat
Ⓜ Cluny la Sorbonne

Artazart (3, H2) This cool Canal St-Martin bookshop specialises in books and magazines on art, photography, visual communications, graphic design, multimedia and web design.
☎ 01 40 40 24 00
🖳 www.artazart.com
✉ 83 quai de Valmy, 10e 🕙 10.30am-7.30pm Mon-Fri, 2-8pm Sat & Sun
Ⓜ Jacques Bonsergent

Les Mots à la Bouche (5, D2) Paris' premier gay bookshop specialises in books written by gay and lesbians regarding queer themes. There are also CDs, videos and magazines, some in English.
☎ 01 42 78 88 30
✉ 6 rue Ste-Croix de la Bretonnerie, 4e
🕙 11am-10pm Mon-Sat, 2-8pm Sun Ⓜ Hôtel de Ville

Librarie Gourmande (5, C3) Considered to be the best food bookshop around, this is the place to come if your obsession with food matches that of the local Parisians. All the classic texts of the culinary arts are here in a mouth-watering shop.
☎ 01 43 54 37 27
✉ 4 rue Dante, 5e
🕙 10am-7pm Mon-Sat
Ⓜ Maubert-Mutualité

Shakespeare and Co (5, C3) Named after Sylvia Beach's bookshop (which published James Joyce's *Ulysses* in 1922, but was shut by the Nazis), this must be Paris' most

Shakespeare as you like it

famous English-language bookshop. It has a varied collection of new and used books in English and other languages, hosts poetry readings and is a meeting spot for young expats.
☎ 01 43 26 96 50 ✉ 37 rue de la Bûcherie, 5e
Ⓜ St-Michel 🕙 noon-midnight

Taschen (5, B2) This sleek black shop has a gallery feel, suitable for

Little histories ready to burst from these items at L'Objet Qui Parle

this arty neighbourhood and the gorgeous Taschen photography, art, architecture, interiors and design books on display.
☎ 01 40 51 79 22
✉ 2 rue de Buci, 6e
🕐 11am-8pm Mon-Sun
Ⓜ Mabillon

WH Smith (3, E2) This is an excellent stop for your holiday reading – the Paris branch of this English chain has a diverse selection of English-language reading material, particularly in the genre of travel books and fiction. There are a couple of massive racks of magazines as well.
☎ 01 44 77 88 99
✉ 248 rue de Rivoli, 1er 🕐 9am-7.30pm Mon-Sat, 1-7.30pm Sun
Ⓜ Concorde

Ulysse (5, D3) For many years Catherine Demain has been fuelling the wanderlust of Parisian travellers in this delightful shop full of travel guides, maps, back issues of *National Geographic* and sage advice.
☎ 01 43 25 17 35
💻 www.ulysse.fr ✉ 26 rue St-Louis en l'Île, 4e 🕐 2-8pm Tue-Sat
Ⓜ Pont Marie

A Shopping Bag Full of Memories

Take home books, music and movies to make those Paris moments all the more memorable:

Books

- *À la Recherche du Temps Perdu* (In Search of Lost Time; Marcel Proust; 1913–27) About the very act of remembering.
- *The Ambassadors* (Henry James; 1903) Best portrait of a *flâneur* in Paris.
- *The Arcades Project* (Walter Benjamin, 1922) Travels through passages in time.
- *The Flâneur* (Edmund White; 2001) A gay take on *flâneurie*.
- *Le Petit Prince* (Antoine de Saint-Exupéry; 1943) The influence of chance meetings.

Film

- *À Bout de Souffle* (Breathless; directed by Jean Luc-Godard; 1959) Paris has never looked as stylish as it does in this revolutionary film!
- *Chacun Cherche son Chat* (When the Cat's Away; directed by Cedri Klapisch; 1996) Fun and games in the Bastille.
- *Eloge de l'Amour* (In Praise of Love; directed by Jean Luc Godard; 2002) Godard's long-awaited return to the city's streets.
- *La Haine* (Hate; directed by Matthieu Kassovitz; 1995) A gritty look at Paris' *banlieues* (suburbs).
- *Notebook on Cities and Clothes* (directed by Wim Winders; 1989) A must for fashion junkies.
- *On Connait La Chanson* (Same Old Song; directed by Alain Resnais; 1997) One for music fans.

Music

- *Café de Paris* (Édith Piaf, Yves Montand, Maurice Chevalier; 2003) Doesn't get more French-sounding than this!
- *Femmes de Paris* (songstresses including Brigitte Bardot, Christie Laume; 2002) Groovy '60s hits.
- *I Love Serge* (various artists; 2002) Electronica's homage to Gainsbourg.
- *Le Flow* (various artists; 2000) The definitive collection of French hip-hop.
- *Sacrebleu* (Dimitri from Paris; 2001) Polyester pop meets acid jazz.

MUSIC

Crocodisc (5, C3) An excellent range of new and used African, Oriental, Caribbean and soul is at this popular shop. There is a small mix of pop and rock, but for jazz and blues try **Crocojazz** (3, G5).
☎ 01 43 54 47 95
✉ 40-42 rue des Écoles, 5e ☽ 11am-7pm Tue-Sat Ⓜ Maubert-Mutualité

FNAC Musique (5, F3) FNAC music is France's largest book and music chain. Its flagship music shop at Bastille has a big choice of local and international music. The

branch at **Les Halles** (3, G3) is well stocked too. The booking desk sells tickets for almost all concerts in Paris – look for the long line of people.
☎ 01 49 54 30 00
🖳 www.fnac.fr ✉ 4 place de la Bastille, 12e ☽ 10am-8pm Mon-Sat, to 10pm Wed Ⓜ Bastille

La Chaumière (5, B4) La Chaumière has a comprehensive catalogue of classical music from all the right labels as well as very knowledgeable staff.
☎ 01 43 54 07 25 ✉ 5 rue de Vaugirard, 6e

☽ 11am-8pm Mon-Sat, 2-8pm Sun Ⓜ Odéon

Virgin Megastore (3, C2) The French-owned version of the multinational chain has the best collection of CDs and DVDs in Paris, as well as English-language books and magazines, and a decent café. The late opening hours keep it very busy.
☎ 01 49 53 50 00
🖳 www.virginmega .fr ✉ 52-60 av des Champs-Élysées, 8e ☽ 10am-midnight Mon-Sat, noon-midnight Sun Ⓜ Franklin D Roosevelt

HOMEWARES & DESIGN

Bains Plus (5, D1) No need to look anywhere else for the fluffiest of bath towels, silky bathrobes, soft cotton slippers, ceramic soap dishes, mirrors and shaving sets. For more pampering, there are oriental *hammam* products such as olive-oil soap, wooden bath clogs and massage oils, as well as creamy body lotions and moisturisers.
☎ 01 48 87 83 07 ✉ 51 rue des Francs-Bourgeois, 4e ☽ 11am-7pm Tue-Sat, 2.30-7pm Sun Ⓜ Hôtel de Ville

E Dehillerin (3, F3) This is a favourite spot with Paris' chefs as well as visiting gourmets. Stepping inside here compares to opening a cluttered kitchen cupboard that is

bursting with the most extraordinary selection of professional-quality cookware.
☎ 01 42 36 53 13 ✉ 18-20 rue Coquillière, 1er ☽ 8am-6pm Mon-Sat (closed 12.30-2pm Mon) Ⓜ Les Halles

Home Trotter (5, F2) This Eastern interiors shop is stocked with contemporary Asian colonial furniture and Zen accessories. There is an abundance of black teak, paper screens and lanterns, intricately patterned cushions, Japanese sandals, Chinese slippers, aromatic candles, incense, chopsticks as well as a display of teapots.
☎ 01 48 06 09 21 ✉ 13 rue Daval, 11e ☽ 10am-7pm (from 2pm Mon) Ⓜ Bastille

Pylônes (4, D3) Announcing itself as 'the French design factory', this place involves local designers to create cutting-edge items such as colourful toasters, plastic juicers and fluffy dusters.
☎ 01 46 06 37 00
✉ 7 rue Tardieu, 18e ☽ 10am-12.30pm & 2-7pm Tue-Sat Ⓜ Abbesses

Sentou Marais (5, D2) This interior shop has innovative furniture, lighting and homeware by Arne Jacobsen, Charles Eames, Vitra, Isamo Noguchi and other designers that make you consider querying your baggage allowance.
☎ 01 42 78 50 60
🖳 www.sentou.fr ✉ 29 rue François Miron, 4e ☽ 11am-2pm & 3-7pm Tue-Fri, 11am-7pm Sat Ⓜ St-Paul

FOOD & DRINK

À l'Olivier (5, D2)
Specialising in olive oils from the Mediterranean, such as Provence and the Peloponnese, this is the place for high-quality oils, olives, vinegars, mustards, spices, pesto and tapenades, kitchen accessories, and olive-oil soaps, cosmetics and fragrances.
☎ 01 48 04 86 59
✉ 23 rue de Rivoli, 4e
⊙ 9.30am-7pm Tue-Sat
Ⓜ St-Paul

Ruffle your tastebuds at Maison de La Truffe (p61)

Dalloyau (3, C2) Dalloyau is to pastries what Poilâne (opposite) is to bread – simply the best. Established in 1802 this venerable patisserie produces the most delicious *croissants au chocolat*, *pain aux raisins*, brioche and *tartes aux pommes*.
☎ 01 42 99 90 00
✉ 101 rue du Faubourg St-Honoré, 8e
⊙ 8.30am-9pm Ⓜ St-Philippe du Roule

Fauchon (3, E2) Paris' finest gourmet department

store sells the most mouth-watering delicacies, from velvety foie gras to tasty patés and exotics preserves, such as rose-petal jam. It's hard to go past the chocolates in sexy hot pink packaging and the elegant tins of fruit jellies though!
☎ 01 47 42 60 11 ✉ 26-30 place de la Madeleine, 8e ⊙ Mon-Sat 8.30am-7pm Ⓜ Madeleine

Hédiard (3, D2) A close rival to Fauchon, this

luxury food store stocks an enormous selection of chocolates, teas, coffees, wines, pâtés, caviar and preserves stacked high to the ceiling. You'll also find pre-prepared dishes at the deli counter, and fresh fruit and vegetables.
☎ 01 43 12 88 88 ✉ 21 place de la Madeleine, 8e ⊙ 9am-9.30pm Mon-Sat, 9am-9pm Sun Ⓜ Madeleine

Le Palais des Thés (5, E1) Desiring a freshness and quality they claimed couldn't be found in Paris, 50 tea enthusiasts got together to establish Le Palais des Thés, travelling around the globe to personally select rare crops from outside the traditional supplier circuit. They also let you try before you buy!
☎ 01 43 56 90 90
🖳 www.palaisdesthes .com ✉ 64 rue Vieille du Temple, 3e ⊙ 10-8pm Mon-Sun Ⓜ St-Paul

Don't Leave Paris Without ...
- An elegant tin of exquisite chocolates from Fauchon (above).
- 'Baume Automobile' facial moisturiser from Detaille (p55).
- Getting your book purchase from Shakespeare and Co imprinted with the store's 'Kilometre Zero Paris' stamp (p57).
- A set of shiny *boules* or regional product from France Ma Douce (p62).
- An Eiffel Tower snow dome from the rue de Rivoli souvenir shops (p50).

JEAN-BERNARD CARILLET

Les Caves Augé (3, D1)
Paris' oldest wine shop was a favourite haunt of Marcel Proust. Now under the stewardship of passionate and knowledgeable sommelier Marc Sibard, the shop presents regular, jovial wine tastings on the pavement outside – they're excellent fun.
☎ 01 45 22 16 97
✉ 116 blvd Haussmann, 8e ☾ 9am-7.30pm Mon-Sat (from 1pm Mon)
Ⓜ St-Augustin

Maison de la Truffe (3, D2) If you're prepared to spend over €300 for 100g of fine French black truffles from Perigord (from late October to March) or Italian Alba

white truffles (from mid-October to December – don't ask the price!) then this is the place to shop. At least take in the heady aromas as you sample delicious truffle dishes at the small sit-down area, open from noon each day.
☎ 01 42 65 53 22
✉ 19-21 place de la Madeleine, 8e ☾ 9am-9pm Mon-Sat (to 8pm Mon) Ⓜ Madeleine

Mariage Frères (5, D2)
Established in 1854, Paris' premier tea shop has around 500 varieties of tea from 32 countries, along with some of the city's best madeleines, and a legendary *crème brûlée* tart. In summer you can cool off

in the 19th-century *salon de thé* with a tea-flavoured ice cream.
☎ 01 42 72 28 11
✉ 30-32 rue du Bourg Tibourg, 4e ☾ 10.30am-7.30pm, tearoom 12-7pm
Ⓜ Hôtel de Ville

Poilâne (3, E5) The perfectly baked Poilâne bread is legendary in Paris and worth queuing up for. Locals are happy to wait because they know that the traditional *pain de campagne* is the most sought after in the city, although *le pain aux noix* is also very popular.
☎ 01 45 48 42 59 ✉ 8 rue du Cherche-Midi, 6e ☾ 7.15am-8.15pm Mon-Sat Ⓜ St-Sulpice

FOR CHILDREN

Apache (2, G4) Every toy imaginable is available at this huge colourful shop that has an Internet café for kids and a regular fun-filled programme of activities, including games, creativity, food and magic, based on themes such as 'Voyage to Africa' to 'Colour'.
☎ 01 53 46 60 10
✉ 84 rue du Faubourg St-Antoine, 12e
☾ 10.30am-6.30pm Mon-Sat Ⓜ Ledru-Rollin

FNAC Junior (3, E6) This kid-oriented branch of the FNAC retail chain has an excellent selection of educational toys, books, videos, CD-ROMs and other multimedia products.
☎ 01 56 24 03 46 ✉ 19 rue Vavin, 6e ☾ 10am-

7.30pm Mon-Sat
Ⓜ Vavin

Gaspard de la Butte (4, D3) Catherine Malaure lovingly sews, knits and crochets her beautiful hand-made children's clothes in her charming store, ensuring you have lots to choose from in her bright-coloured collections – unusual graphic patterns, lollypop colours, and exquisite attention to detail are her hallmarks.
☎ 01 42 55 99 40
✉ 10bis rue Yvonne Le Tac, 18e ☾ 10am-7pm Tue-Sun Ⓜ Abbesses

Pain-de'Épices (3, F2)
Although this delightful store specialises in miniature dolls, clothes,

furniture and accessories for doll houses, you'll also find traditional toys such as puppets, sailing boats, wooden toys, and traditional games.
☎ 01 47 70 08 68 ✉ 29-31 passage Jouffroy, 9e ☾ 10am-7pm Tue-Sat (to 9pm Thu), 12.30-7pm Mon Ⓜ Grands Boulevards

Si Tu Veux (3, F2) Packed to the brim with high-quality traditional toys, creative kits and innovative activities for children, this is probably Paris' best toy shop. It's certainly the most whimsical.
☎ 01 42 60 59 97 ✉ 68 Galerie Vivienne, 2e ☾ 10.30am-7pm Mon-Sat Ⓜ Bourse

SPECIALIST STORES

Belle de Jour (4, D3) If you can pull your nose away from the window display of this Montmartre shop, take your olfactory senses inside where you can sniff at the aromas that still waft from the exquisite collection of colourful and rare perfume bottles.

☎ 01 46 06 15 28
✉ 7 rue Tardieu, 18e
🕐 10am-12.30pm & 2-7pm Tue-Sat Ⓜ Abbesses

Espace Michelin (3, F3) The tubby white Michelin man waves at you from an enormous array of well-made gifts and gadgets such as key rings, pens, torches, lighters, watches, T-shirts, soft toys, trucks and cars, pocket knives, compasses, travel clocks, books and guides, but we're particularly fond of the chef's apron.

☎ 01 42 68 05 00 ✉ 32 avenue de l'Opéra, 1e
🕐 10am-7pm Mon-Sat
Ⓜ Pyramides

France Ma Douce (5, D2) This shop specialises in high-quality French regional products, highlighting the best of each province. Ceramics, pottery, hand-blown glass pitchers, scented candles, linen, hand-made soaps, lavender perfume, honey and olive oil all make for outstanding original souvenirs.

☎ 01 44 59 38 03 ✉ 27 rue du Bourg Tibourg, 4e Ⓜ Hotel de Ville
🕐 9am-8pm Mon-Sat (2-8pm Sun)

Le Prince Jardinier (3, F3) Who'll resist the gardening clothes and items fit for a king or a weekend farmer? It sells quality linen work shirts, pants and overalls, straw sun hats, aprons, flower baskets, tool belts and shiny watering cans.

☎ 01 42 60 37 13
🖥 www.princejardinier .fr ✉ 37 rue de Valois, Arcades du Palais Royal, 1er 🕐 10am-7pm Mon-Sat Ⓜ Palais Royal

Les Archives de la Presse (5, D1) Step back in time and see the gorgeous young things of the '60s and '70s – Brigitte Bardot, Catherine Deneuve, Jane Birkin and Elizabeth Taylor – smile from the groovy *Vogue* and *Elle* covers at this fabulous shop specialising in old magazines and newspapers. ☎ 01 42 72 63 93 ✉ 51 rue des Archives, 3e
🕐 10am-7pm Mon-Sat
Ⓜ Rambuteau

Litchi (5, D2) An effervescent collection of kitsch religious trinkets and good-luck charms from around the globe awaits you at Litchi. Expect psychedelic wall hangings and postcards of Indian gods and goddesses, little Buddha statues, Mexican Day of the Dead paraphernalia, Brazilian Santeria wrist ties, Orthodox icons, and Chinese waterlily candles.

☎ 01 44 59 39 09
🖥 www.litchi.com
✉ 4 rue des Écouffes, 4e
🕐 12am-8pm Tue-Sat, 1.30-7pm Sun Ⓜ St-Paul

Stern (3, F2) At this elegant old-fashioned shop you can have your own personalised stationery designed. Take a seat for a consultation to select from an enormous range of business cards, letterhead, note paper and 'with compliments' slips in classical styles.

☎ 01 45 08 86 45 ✉ 47 Passage des Panoramas, 2e 🕐 7.30am-12.30pm & 1.30-5.30pm Mon-Sat (to 12.30pm Thu & Sat) Ⓜ Grands Boulevards

---

Late-Night Shopping

Paris is not a 24-hour city but if you crave a snack late at night go to the revamped **Drugstore Publicis** (3, B1; ☎ 01 44 43 79 00; 131 av des Champs Élysées, 8e; 🕐 10am-2am; Ⓜ Charles de Gaulle-Étoile) – an institution since 1958 and former haunt of Serge Gainsbourg, Catherine Deneuve and the Aga Khan – for gourmet groceries, wine, cigars, gifts, cosmetics, newspapers and books. If you want a snack, bread or pastries try **Boulangerie de l'Ancienne Comédie** (5, B3; ☎ 01 43 26 89 7210; rue de l'Ancienne Comédie, 6e; 🕐 24hr; Ⓜ Odéon).

Eating

The gastronomic history of Paris weighed heavily on its Gallic shoulders until recently. The cosmopolitan dining scenes of both New York and Sydney had exposed Paris' culinary time warp. Paris was filled with stuffy *haute cuisine* establishments and bistros with lacklustre *prix fixe* (fixed-price) menus that could have been set in stone rather than scribbled on a blackboard. In recent years chefs Pierre Gagnaire (p66) has impressed all with his poetic plates, über-talented Hélène Darroze's (p75) take on 'tapas' has neatly updated southwestern French cuisine and bistros such as L'Epi Dupin (p74) has calmed the fear of the *prix fixe* menu.

There were more eateries to try, but also more to gossip about, for Parisians love discussing food! Well, except for breakfast. *Petit déjeuner*, literally 'little lunch', is a croissant or a baguette with jam and a quick coffee. *Déjeuner* (lunch) is often the main meal of the day in Paris and many Parisians head for a restaurant rather than eat at work. Restaurants are generally open from noon to 2.30pm for lunch and from 7pm to 11pm for *dîner* (dinner or supper), while brasseries are open from 11am to midnight. Many restaurants are closed either for the weekend or Sunday and Monday and the better ones are generally closed in August.

There are various 'French cuisine' types – each based on the produce and gastronomy of the individual *provinces* (regions) of France. Paris doesn't have a strong individual cuisine; its chefs reinterpret regional classics and are inspired by the cuisine of its ethnically mixed neighbourhoods. The cuisine of the successive waves of immigrants from France's former colonies and protectorates – particularly Africa, and the Middle East – are now a permanent feature of Paris' dining scene.

Le Salon d'Hélène – now that's art (p75)

JEAN-BERNARD CARILLET

BASTILLE & FAUBOURG ST-ANTOINE

Blue Elephant
(3, J4) $$
Thai
While this worldwide chain is expanding, the food at this branch hasn't suffered. The refined Thai cooking is authentic – try the Plateau Royal Blue Elephant (€25.50) for starters if there's a group of you. There's a good vegetarian menu and check the little red elephants on the menu that indicate spicy dishes – they take their heat seriously here!
☎ 01 47 00 42 00
🖳 www.blueelephant
.com ✉ 43 rue de la Roquette, 11e 🕙 noon-2.30pm Mon-Fri, noon-3pm Sun & 7pm-midnight Mon-Sat, to 11pm Sun
Ⓜ Bastille Ⓥ

Brasserie Bofinger
(5, F2) $$$
Brasserie
One of Paris' oldest and buzziest brasseries, this original Art Nouveau wonder exemplifies Parisian brasserie dining. While there seems to be enormous seafood or *choucroute* (sauerkraut) platters on every table, don't let that stop you from taking the *prix-fixe* menu (€30.50), which includes a half-bottle of wine. Book ahead for a table under the beautiful downstairs glass cupola.
☎ 01 42 72 87 82
🖳 www.bofingerparis
.com ✉ 5-7 rue de la Bastille, 4e 🕙 noon-3pm & 6.30pm-1am Mon-Fri, noon-1am Sat & Sun
Ⓜ Bastille

L'Ébauchoir
(2, H4) $$
Bistro
This convivial workers' eatery attracts a loyal local clientele who mix it with the hipsters who have recently unearthed it. The usual bistro food is well-prepared but dishes like marinated herrings and veal liver with honey sauce draws in customers.
☎ 01 43 42 49 31
✉ 45 rue de Cîteaux, 12e 🕙 noon-2.30pm & 8-11pm Mon-Sat
Ⓜ Faidherbe Chaligny

L'Écailler du Bistrot
(2, H4) $$
Seafood Bistro
Oyster lovers must go *tout suite* (at once) to this seaside-kitsch bistro that has up to a dozen options of fresh bivalve molluscs on the blackboard. The freshly shucked oysters are served with a little lemon and other seafood delights are given equal respect, such as minute-cooked tuna steak with sesame oil. The excellent *formule* lunch (usually €15) includes oysters.
☎ 01 43 72 76 77
✉ 22 rue Paul-Bert, 11e 🕙 noon-2.30pm Tue-Sat, 7.30-11.30pm Mon-Sat
Ⓜ Faidherbe Chaligny

Le Square Trousseau
(2, G4) $$
Bistro
While this place has been attracting runway types and fashionistas for some time, thankfully the *menu* hasn't turned to sushi to cater for them. The home-made foie gras is a delight and main course chicken dishes are worth trying, while the gorgeous *belle époque* interior and the amiable staff make you forget that Gaultier has just left the building.
☎ 01 43 43 06 00 ✉ 1 rue Antoine Vollon, 12e 🕙 11.30am-2pm & 7-10.30pm Ⓜ Ledru Rollin

Le Train Bleu
(3, J6) $$$
Brasserie
Until recently, the food was no match for the majestic *belle époque* interior of this wonderful dining room upstairs at Gare de Lyon. With the kitchen now run by respected chef André Signoret, you can sample classic French fare worthy of the room (a listed monument) or drink in the scene from the comfy bar.
☎ 01 53 80 24 00
🖳 www.le-train-bleu
.com ✉ 26 pl Louis Armand, Gare de Lyon, 12e 🕙 11.30am-3pm & 7-11pm Ⓜ Gare de Lyon

Swann & Vincent
(3, J5) $$
Italian
While much of Paris' Italian food is exasperatingly inauthentic, this earthy Italian eatery is the real deal. Excellent breads, fresh pasta and a decent tiramisu keep the place busy for lunch and dinner.
☎ 01 43 43 49 40
✉ 7 rue St-Nicolas, 12e 🕙 noon-2.45pm & 7.30-11.45pm Sun-Wed, 7.30pm-12.15am Thu-Sat
Ⓜ Ledru Rollin Ⓥ

BUTTES AUX CAILLES & CHINATOWN

**L'Avant-Goût
(2, F5)** $$
Modern French
Chef Christophe Beaufront's
reputation is such that
he could have a chain of
bistros by now. Thankfully
his wife still greets you at
the door and the market-
fresh contemporary cuisine
is as finely tuned as ever.
Although it's still a casual
bistro, book ahead and ask
if the signature *pot-au-feu
de cochon* (pig casserole) is
on the menu.
☎ 01 53 80 24 00
✉ 26 rue Bobillot, 13e
🕑 noon-2pm & 7.30-
11pm Tue-Fri Ⓜ Place
d'Italie

**Le Temps des Cérises
(2, F6)** $
French
This 'anarchistic' restaurant
run by a workers' cooper-
ative remains a favourite
due to its convivial atmos-
phere and unpretentious
fare. Stick to the straight-
forward *menu* items (such as

Menu v. Menu
Most restaurants offer you the choice of ordering
à la carte (from the *menu*) or ordering one fixed-
price, multicourse meal known in French as a *menu*
or *prix fixe*. This allows you to pick two out of three
courses (eg starter and main course or main course
and dessert). A *menu* generally costs much less than
ordering à la carte. Where more than one *menu* price
is listed, the cheaper is normally only available at
lunchtime. Sometimes a *formule* is offered, usually
a much reduced choice *prix fixe* menu. Often more
difficult-to-prepare dishes are only found on the
dinner menu.

steak frites), order a carafe of
house wine and soak up the
old-fashioned charm.
☎ 01 45 89 69 48 ✉ 18-
20 rue de la Buttes aux
Cailles, 13e 🕑 11.45am-
2pm & 7.30-11.30pm
Mon-Fri, 7.30pm-midnight
Sat Ⓜ Corvisart

**Tricotin
(2, G6)** $
Asian
If you're venturing deep
into the heart of China-

town, Tricotin offers two
dining areas to satisfy a
craving for Asian fare. On
the left side is Thai and
Malaysian offering decent
Thai curries while the one
on the right side does a
roaring trade with its duck
dishes and soups.
☎ 01 45 85 51 52 (Thai
restaurant), 01 45 84 74
44 (Asian restaurant)
✉ 15 av de Choisy, 13e
🕑 9am-11pm Ⓜ Porte
de Choisy ♿ Ⓥ

Wall-to-wall clientele and stomachs full to the brim – that's Tricotin

CHAMPS ÉLYSÉES

Alain Ducasse au Plaza Athénée
(3, B2) $$$$
Haute Cuisine
Ducasse, one of France's best *haute cuisine* chefs, received three Michelin stars only five months after opening his flagship restaurant while some chefs spend their whole careers chasing one. From your first sip of champagne to your wobbly exit it's a blur of fantastic service, extraordinary flavours, endless plates and an astonishing bill. Order one of the *dégustation* menus.
☎ 01 53 67 65 00
🖥 www.alain-ducasse .com ✉ Hôtel Plaza Athénée, 25 ave de Montaigne, 8e ⏱ noon-2pm Thu-Fri & 7-9pm Mon-Fri Ⓜ Alma-Marceau

Guy Savoy
(3, B1) $$$$
Haute Cuisine
Star chef Guy Savoy may run an empire, but he's a constant presence at his smartly revamped signature restaurant. Guy's deft touch shows in his now classic starters; *soupe d'artichaut à la truffle noire* (artichoke soup with black truffles) and *huîtres en nage glacée* (oyster jelly served with a fresh oyster) and a vanilla millefeuille. Book well ahead.
☎ 01 43 80 40 61
🖥 www.guysavoy .com ✉ 18 rue Troyon, 17e ⏱ 12.30-2.30pm & 7-10.30pm Tue-Fri, 7-10.30pm Sat Ⓜ Charles de Gaulle-Etoile

Le Bistrot du Sommelier
(3, D1) $$$$
French
Owner Philippe Faure-Brac was Meilleur Sommelier du Monde in 1992 and the best way to try his wine–food matchings is by ordering a *dégustation* menu (from €60-100, including wine). The food is hearty French fare and surprisingly not all the wines might be French.
☎ 01 42 65 24 85
🖥 www.bistrotdusom melier.com ✉ 97 blvd Haussmann, 8e ⏱ noon-2.30pm & 7.30-11pm Mon-Fri Ⓜ St-Augustin

Market
(3, C2) $$$
Contemporary
Culinary hipster Jean-Georges Vongerichten's Paris restaurant specialises in fresh market produce with Asian-influenced eclectic combinations. While it's less formal than his American restaurants, it's a refined experience with lunch wooing a business crowd, and dinner a sexier affair.
☎ 01 56 43 40 90
🖥 www.jean-georges .com ✉ 15 ave Matignon, 8e ⏱ noon-3pm & 7.30-11.30pm Sun-Tue, 7.30pm-12.30am Wed-Sat, brunch 8-11am Mon-Fri Ⓜ Franklin D Roosevelt

Pierre Gagnaire
(3, B1) $$$$
Haute Cuisine
Gagnaire's frequently changing menus reflect seasonal produce and his painterly presentation and flavour combinations are now legendary. No matter which menu you choose (the *prix fixe* menu is recommended) make sure to try his signature *le grand dessert Pierre Gagnaire* – simply the seven wonders of desserts.
☎ 01 58 36 12 50
🖥 www.pierre-gagnaire .com ✉ 6 rue Balzac, 8e ⏱ noon-2pm & 7-10pm Mon-Fri, 7-10pm Sun Ⓜ Charles de Gaulle-Étoile

JEAN-BERNARD CARILLET

Go to Alain Ducasse for a seriously Michelin-star experience

JEAN-BERNARD CARILLET

From market to Market

Spoon Food & Wine
(3, C2) $$$
International
Alain Ducasse (opposite) takes you on a whimsical culinary journey at his less formal eatery. Delicious pan-seared beef with barbecue sauce and BLT (bacon, lettuce and tomato) is as inviting as chicken fillet with Tandoori gravy. If Ducasse shocked Paris with the menu (including bubblegum ice cream and homemade cookies), he left it apoplectic by including New World wines on *la carte*.
☎ 01 40 76 34 44
🖳 www.spoon.tm.fr
✉ 14 rue de Marignan, 8e ⏱ noon-2pm & 7-11pm Mon-Fri Ⓜ Franklin D Roosevelt Ⓥ

Taillevent
(3, B1) $$$$
Haute Cuisine
This mainstay of Paris' *haute cuisine* scene is also its most reliable under the steady leadership of Jean-Claude Vrinat. With revamped décor and pedigreed chef Alain Solivérès on board, the place could well boast another thirty years of Michelin's highest rating. Tackle a tasting menu (€70 – lunch only, €130 or €180), which features some of the Basque-influenced touches of Solivérès, and rely on the excellent staff recommendations for matching wines.
☎ 01 44 95 15 01
🖳 www.taillevent.com
✉ 15 rue Lamennais, 8e ⏱ noon-2pm & 7.30-10pm Mon-Fri Ⓜ Charles de Gaulle-Étoile

GRANDS BOULEVARDS

Aux Lyonnais
(3, F2) $$$
Bistro
As with Moissonnier (p79), this glorious bistro serves to highlight the wonderful cuisine of Lyon. The concise, seasonal menu features hearty salads and all of the menu items based on *cochon* (pig) come with an ironclad guarantee to satisfy. Everything seems to tastes better with lashings of Beaujolais – the *vin* that complements the food best.
☎ 01 42 96 65 04; fax 01 42 97 42 95 ✉ 32 rue Saint-Marc, 2e ⏱ noon-2pm & 7.30-10pm Mon-Fri Ⓜ Bourse

Chartier
(3, F2) $
French
One of the last of Paris' *bouillons* (cafés that offer filling soups to ordinary folks) this place feels like being time-tunnelled back to the early 20th century. No doubt the menu hasn't altered for years, but it's perfect nosh for a rainy day. The décor is a treat (check the brass hat racks!) but the cacophony of a lunch in full swing is full-on.
☎ 01 47 70 86 29 ✉ 7 rue du Faubourg Montmartre, 9e ⏱ 11.30-3pm & 6-10pm Ⓜ Charles de Gaulle-Étoile

Le Général Lafayette
(3, F1) $$
Bistro
With its all-day menu, *belle époque* décor and Belgian beers, this is the place to go if you're hungry outside usual dining hours. Try classics, such as onion soup and crisp duck *confit* with potatoes.
☎ 01 47 70 59 08
✉ 52 rue Lafayette, 9e ⏱ 10am-4am Ⓜ Poissonière

Le Grand Colbert
(3, F2) $$$
Brasserie
Since its scene-stealer in the film, *Something's Gotta Give*,

this place is wooing new and old fans to its service and trusty meals. The herrings are great and the *côte de bœuf* (steak) is ample. Jack Nicholson and Diane Keaton's table needs to be booked a month ahead.

☎ 01 42 86 87 88
✉ 2-4 rue Vivienne, 2e
🕙 noon-3pm & 7pm-1am Ⓜ Bourse

Velly
(3, F1) $$
Bistro
The eclectic mix of locals that come to this tiny bistro know

they're on to a good thing. With an often-changing menu, order what sounds appealing – it's all fresh produce, well cooked and well presented. There's a short but sweet wine list.

☎ 01 48 78 60 05
✉ 52 rue Lamartine, 9e 🕙 noon-2.30pm & 7.45-10.30pm Ⓜ Notre-Dame-de-Lorette

Wally le Saharien
(3, F1) $$$
Moroccan
This establishment is a longstanding favourite in

an increasingly crowded North African dining scene in Paris. At lunchtime you can order à la carte, but dinner (which is highly recommended) is a *carte-free* zone with everybody relishing the *prix fixe* menu (€40.40). Pigeon pastilla as well as the exquisite couscous and tasty merguez sausages follow a delicious harira soup.

☎ 01 42 85 51 90
✉ 36 rue Rodier, 9e
🕙 noon-2.30pm & 7.30-10.30pm Tue-Sat
Ⓜ St-Georges Ⓥ

LOUVRE & LES HALLES

Au Pied de Cochon
(3, F3) $$$
French gastronomic tradition dictates using all of the animal, so if you're a dedicated carnivore order *Pied de Cochon Grillé Sauce Béarnaise* (grilled pig trotter with Béarnaise sauce). For those who don't fancy facing a plate full of pig, other specialities (such as the oysters) are excellent.

☎ 01 40 13 77 00
🖳 www.piedde cochon.com ✉ 6 rue Coquillières, 1er 🕙 24hr
Ⓜ Les Halles

Café Marly
(5, A1) $$$
Modern French
Sipping a glass of champagne under the colonnades of the Louvre while in front of the glass

pyramid is a classic Parisian experience. Your attention may be drawn elsewhere as the citizen-to-celebrity ratio weighs heavily in the supermodels favour. The food is too self-consciously contemporary and no match for the view.

☎ 01 46 26 06 60
✉ 93 rue de Rivoli, 1e
🕙 11am-1am Ⓜ Palais Royal

For a post-Louvre pick-me-up, head for Café Marly

JEAN-BERNARD CARILLET

Chez Georges
(3, F2) $$$
Bistro

This eatery covers all Parisian bistro desires – a convivial feel, warm service and great food. The long mirrored room fills quickly for lunch and dinner with families, old friends and business buddies who know the timeless menu by heart. Foie gras, escargots and steak with Béarnaise sauce are worth trying. If the profiteroles were off the dessert menu, there'd be a revolution.

☎ 01 42 60 07 11 ✉ 1 rue du Mail, 2e ⏱ noon-2pm & 7 9.30pm Mon-Sat Ⓜ Bourse ⑤

Georges
(5, D1) $$$
International

This wonderful space has a brilliant view from the top of Centre Pompidou if you're offered a good table by the nonchalant staff. Once seated, though, you could be forgiven for wondering what the fuss is about. The food is international but not exciting enough to distract you from the view for too long.

☎ 01 44 78 47 99 ✉ Centre Pompidou, 6th fl, rue Rambuteau, 4e ⏱ noon-2am Ⓜ Rambuteau

L'Absinthe
(3, E2) $$$
Bistro

Being close to the financial district means you'll be lunching with suits, but its stylish bistro fare and (weather permitting) outdoor seating make it worthwhile. There's an extensive wine list and although it's

Chez George *très delicious*

one of chef Michel Rostang's many bistros at least it's run by his daughter.

☎ 01 49 26 90 04 ⌨ www.michelrostang .com ✉ 24 place du Marché St-Honoré, 1er ⏱ noon-2.15pm Mon-Fri & 7.30-11pm Mon-Sat Ⓜ Tuileries

Le Dauphin
(5, C1) $$$
Bistro

The pedigreed chefs left lovely Biarritz on the southwest coast to bring some Basque flavour to this bistro in central Paris. There are two hard-to-choose routes thorugh the menu, one being the wonderful rustic starters (such as a tuna *confit*) that are shared with excellent bread, and the other being irresistible combinations of classic Spanish *parrillada* (mixed grill).

☎ 01 42 60 40 11 ✉ 1 rue St-Honoré, 1e ⏱ noon-2.30pm & 7.30-10.30pm Ⓜ Pyramides

Noshing with Nippers

Most restaurants in Paris don't have highchairs, children's menus or children's portions. Children are rarely seen in Parisian restaurants – just as well given all the secondhand smoke on offer. While we've mentioned restaurants where the little ones won't be treated as social outcasts using the (⑤) symbol, sadly this is where the North American chain restaurants and its European counterparts (such as Quick, with its serviceable burgers and excellent fries) fill the void.

MARAIS & ST-PAUL

404
(3, H3) $$$
Moroccan
404 serves some of the best couscous and *tajine* (stew) in Paris in a faux-Moroccan atmospheric space (like the owner's Momo in London). The servings are huge, the tables tight and if you're wondering why all the beautiful people are here, they've a date with a *shisha* pipe next door at hip Andy Wahloo (p83). Weekend brunch is recommended.
☎ 01 42 74 57 81 ✉ 69 rue des Gravilliers, 3e ◷ noon-2.30pm, to 4pm Sat & Sun & 8pm-midnight Ⓜ Arts et Métiers

Baracane
(5, F2) $$
Bistro
At night this family-run bistro is bustling with locals and tourists for the capable southwestern provincial cooking. Duck features heavily – try the *foie gras de canard* and the *magret de canard* (fillet of duck breast). Wines include some great southwestern specials.
☎ 01 42 71 43 33 ✉ 38 rue des Tournelles, 4e ◷ noon-2.30pm Mon-Fri & 7pm-midnight Mon-Sat Ⓜ Chemin Vert

Chez Marianne
(5, D2) $$
Jewish
Easily the pick of Jewish eateries in the Marais, Chez Marianne is really a sit-down deli where you choose an *assiette composée*, a selection of salads and hot snacks. The mainly Middle Eastern and North African cuisine is tasty – the breads, salads and falafel are standouts.
☎ 01 42 72 18 86 ✉ 2 rue des Hospitaliéres St-Gervais, 4e ◷ 11am-midnight Ⓜ St-Paul Ⓥ

Chez Omar
(3, H3) $$
North African
No longer flavour-of-the-month with fashionistas, it's a pleasure to not have to stare down supermodels to get a table. While Omar's décor is decidedly French café, the attraction here is couscous and homemade merguez sausages. The servings are huge, the service friendly, there's a good short wine list and they still don't take bookings, but the wait for the table is worth it.
☎ 01 42 72 36 26 ✉ 47 rue de Bretange, 3e ◷ noon-2.30pm & 7.30-11.30pm Ⓜ Arts et Métiers

L'Ambroisie
(5, E2) $$$$
Haute Cuisine
This stunning townhouse on the beautiful place des Vosges is Bernard Pacaud's thrice-starred gastronomic temple. It's all hushed reverence and the service is overly formal for most tastes. The food, however, is mouthwatering in its ingredients, cooking and presentation, although the wine list will make your credit card break out in a cold sweat.
☎ 01 42 78 51 45 ✉ 9 place des Vosges,

Double-strength dose of Frenchness at Chez Omar

JEAN-BERNARD CARILLET

4e ⏲ noon-1.30pm
& 8-9.30pm Tue-Sat
Ⓜ Bastille

L'Enoteca
(5, E3) $$$
Italian
This elegant trattoria
offers great Italian food to
accompany an extensive
list of excellent Italian
wines. The antipasti are
delectable and dishes such
as risotto with Gorgonzola
and pears will transport
you from the Marais to
Milan in no time.
☎ 01 42 78 91 44
✉ 25 rue Charles V,
4e ⏲ noon-2.30pm &
7.30-11.30pm Ⓜ Pont
Marie Ⓥ

Le Petit Marché
(5, E2) $$
Bistro
A great little bistro near the
place des Vosges that fills
up late in the evening with
a mixed crowd who come
to enjoy the hearty cooking
and friendly service. The
salad starters are popular
and the duck breast with
ginger is great, but the
open kitchen is in less
safe territory with more
adventurous fare.
☎ 01 42 72 06 67
✉ 9 rue de Béarn, 3e
⏲ noon-3pm & 8pm
midnight Ⓜ Chemin Vert

Le Réconfort
(3, H3) $$
Bistro
With its well-spaced
tables, ethnic lounge
music and subtle lighting,
the 'Comfort' is not your
average bistro and like
Le Petit Marché (above)
attracts a mixed crowd. It's

also another bistro where
straying too far from the
standards is fine for starters
and desserts but not the
main course.
☎ 01 42 76 06 36
✉ 37 rue de Poitou, 3e
⏲ noon-2pm & 8-11pm
Mon-Sat Ⓜ Filles du
Calvaire

Ma Bourgogne
(5, E2) $$
Bistro
With its enviable position
overlooking place des
Vosges, this cosy bistro
set under the arcades is
a popular one. While the
bistro fare is competent,
the house special of *steak
tartare* (raw finely chopped
meat mixed with egg yolk,
onions and herbs) is delicious and it's a great place
to share a bottle of wine

and watch the passing
parade.
☎ 01 42 78 44 64 ✉ 19
place des Vosges, 4e
⏲ noon-1am Ⓜ St-Paul

Robert et Louise
(5, E1) $$
French
If your notion of France
includes the country inn
complete with red gingham
curtains you don't have to
leave Paris to experience it.
This delightful little place
serves up dishes cooked
over an open fire by a
husband-and-wife team.
Try the *côte de bœuf* for
two with a bottle of Côte
du Rhône.
☎ 01 42 78 55 89 ✉ 64
rue Vieille du Temple, 3e
⏲ noon-2.30pm
& 7-10pm Mon-Sat
Ⓜ St-Sébastien Froissart

I Know The Perfect Place...
Spoilt for choice? Here's a list of favourites to suit
every occasion.
- **Business Lunch** Market (p66)
- **Brasserie Blowout** Brasserie Bofinger (p64)
- **Romantic Dinner** L'Astrance (p80)
- **Fair Weather (with) Friends** Café Marly (p68)
- **Haute Cuisine** Pierre Gagnaire (p66)
- **Will sir/madame be dining alone?** L'Atelier
  de Joël Robuchon (p74)
- **Late night** Brasserie Flo (p72)

JEAN-BERNARD CARILLET

MONTMARTRE, PIGALLE & NORTHERN PARIS

Brasserie Flo
(3, G2) $$$
Brasserie
The first of Jean-Paul Bucher's bistros in the Flo group, its late opening hours make it a Parisian favourite. Inside, the Alsatian woods and smoke-stained murals make it comfortable as does the friendly service. You're best rewarded if you order classics such as oysters and *choucroute* and just sit back and soak up the ambience.
☎ 01 47 70 13 59
🖳 www.floparis.com
✉ 7 cour des Petites Ecuries, 10e 🕑 noon-3pm & 7pm-1.30am
Ⓜ Château d'Eau

Chez Casimir
(2, F2) $$
Bistro
Chez Michel's (right) little brother is a casual affair, but the food, offering less Brittany flavours than its big brother, is still delicious. The fish soup (served in a jug), is an aromatic delight, the mains are earthy and desserts are rich.
☎ 01 48 78 28 80 ✉ 6 rue de Belzunce, 10e
🕑 noon-2pm Mon-Fri & 7-11pm Mon-Sat Ⓜ Gare du Nord

Chez Michel
(2, F2) $$$
Bistro
Chef Thierry Bretton certainly hasn't developed a following because of the décor of this kitschly-adorned eatery; it's his gutsy, seasonal sensations that make bookings essential. Try items from the long specials board – the seasonal game is especially good. Regulars plan for dessert, the *tarte tatin* of apples and quince and the rice pudding are both divine.
☎ 01 44 53 06 20 ✉ 10 rue de Belzunce, 10e,
🕑 noon-2pm Tue-Fri & 7-midnight Mon-Fri Ⓜ Gare du Nord, Poissonnière

Julien
(3, G2) $$
Brasserie
Entering this classic brasserie is a trip back in time to when men wore hats and the neighbourhood wasn't so dodgy. But once inside, you're in safe hands. If you can take your eyes off the magnificent stained glass and beautiful murals, the classics and the *prix fixe* menus (€23.50/€33.50) are excellent and include wine. It's a good late-night choice.
☎ 01 47 70 12 06
🖳 www.julienparis.com in French ✉ 16 rue du Faubourg Saint-Denis, 10e
🕑 noon-3pm & 7pm-1am Ⓜ Strasbourg St-Denis

La Table d'Anvers
(4, E3) $$$
Modern French
Just far enough off the Montmartre tourist track to keep the hordes away, this local favourite offers up some great dishes and a decent *prix fixe* lunch menu (€33). It's an unusual menu with Italian and Provençal influences, and the desserts and cheeses are excellent.
☎ 01 48 78 35 21
✉ 2 place d'Anvers, 9e 🕑 noon-2pm Tue-Fri & 7-11pm Mon-Sat
Ⓜ Anvers

Julien – the perfect place to pop a cork

JEAN-BERNARD CARILLET

MONTPARNASSE

Aquarius
(2, D5) $

Vegetarian

This is the best of Paris' few dedicated vegetarian restaurants. While there's a filling range of dishes for committed vegans, overall it's a little bland considering the potential of Paris' markets. The service and desserts are excellent.

☎ 01 45 41 36 88
✉ 40 rue de Gergovie, 14e ⏲ noon-2.30pm & 7-10.30pm Mon-Sat
Ⓜ Plaisance Ⓥ

Le Dôme
(3, E6) $$$

Seafood

The gorgeous Art Deco interior, the historic patronage, the wonderful seafood – there's plenty to like about this bistro. Try the seafood soup, the shellfish platters are fresh, or the house speciality, *sole meunière* (sole fillets floured and cooked in butter and lemon). There's also an atmospheric café section.

☎ 01 43 35 25 81

Amber-lit ambience at Le Dôme

JONATHAN SMITH

✉ 108 blvd de Montparnasse, 14e ⏲ noon-3pm & 7-12.30pm, café 8am-1.30am Ⓜ Vavin

Natacha
(3, E6) $$$

Modern French

Chef Alain Cirelli has attracted a celebrity crowd to this alluring two-floored space with his updated Parisian favourites. The mushroom ravioli with truffle oil is delicious and game (in season) is a firm favourite. It is one of the only places in town where you'll catch a celebrity ordering a cottage pie.

☎ 01 43 20 79 27 ✉ 7 bis, rue Campagne-Première, 14e ⏲ noon-2.30pm & 8-11.30pm, brunch 11am-4pm Sun Ⓜ Raspail

Je Suis Végétarien

It's easy to feel somewhat neglected as a vegetarian traveller in Paris. Exclusively vegetarian eateries are rare and while some places have vegetarian dishes on the menu, the French love of stocks based on chicken and red meat make these a dicey proposition.

On the positive side of the vegetarian ledger, most North African and Middle Eastern restaurants have some meatless dishes on the menu. There are a handful of Indian restaurants to choose from, with passage Brady (3, G2) in the 10e chock-full of subcontinental restaurants and goodies.

A couple of good options where vegetarians can find decent meals are Aquarius (above), Les Quatre et Une Saveurs (p79)

Other restaurants marked with the (Ⓥ) symbol offer reliable, tasty vegetarian options.

ODÉON & ST-GERMAIN

Brasserie Lipp
(5, A2) $$$
Brasserie
One of Paris' Left Bank in-stitutions, Lipp is legendary for its famous clientele and its reputation for sending unfamiliar faces to dining Siberia (upstairs or at the back of the dining room). It's a little friendlier these days and the food's improved with decent *choucroute garni* and excellent steaks.
☎ 01-45-48-53-91 ✉ 151 blvd St-Ger-main, 6e ⏱ 9am-2am, restaurant service 11am-1am Ⓜ St-Germain des Prés

L'Atelier de Joël Robuchon
(5, A2) $$
Contemporary
Tapas meets sushi and a no bookings policy were most unexpected from the return of France's favourite *haute cuisine* chef. But anchovies with eggplant *confit* are

perfect tapas-size – too rich for a full serve, but enough to whet your appetite for more from the interesting menu. The casual feel is refreshing considering the level of the cuisine.
☎ 01 42 22 56 56 ✉ 5 rue de Montalembert, 7e ⏱ 11.30am-3pm & 6.30pm-midnight Ⓜ Rue du Bac

L'Epi Dupin
(3, E5) $$
Bistro
A victim of its own success, it's hard to get a booking at this *petit bistro* and the waiters have had to learn a little English to cope with the sea-change in clientele. The inventive menu uses produce such as pigeon and rabbit to great effect, and the desserts are delectable. Getting the table you booked, however, can be a frustrating experience.
☎ 01 42 22 64 56 ✉ 11 rue Dupin, 6e

⏱ noon-2.30pm Tue-Fri & 7-10.30pm Mon-Fri Ⓜ Sèvres-Babylone ♿

Le Petit Zinc
(5, A2) $$$
French
Pretty as a picture, this is one of Paris' most romantic and nostalgic spots to dine. The regional southwest French specialities are excellent – try the calf's liver or the lamb (gener-ally served for two). The excellent *crème brûlée* with ginger will end the meal on a sweet note.
☎ 01 42 61 20 60 🖳 www.petit-zinc.com ✉ 11 rue St-Benoît, 6e ⏱ noon-2am Ⓜ St-Germain des Prés

Le Récamier
(3, E4) $$$
French
With its serious suit crowd and moneyed dinner patrons, you could easily dismiss this rather reserved

L'Atelier de Joël Robuchon – bring a cool outfit and attitude

JONATHAN SMITH

restaurant. The well-heeled locals know their food. It's all traditional stuff – but exemplary versions of old-fashioned favourites like *bœuf bourguignon* (beef stew with red wine) keep patrons happy.

☎ 01 45 48 86 58
✉ 11 rue Récamier, 7e 🕑 noon-2.30pm & 7-10.30pm Mon-Sat 🅜 Sèvres-Babylone

Le Salon d'Hélène
(3, E5) $$$$
Contemporary French
While culinary star Hélène Darroze has a fine dining restaurant upstairs (awarded two Michelin stars), this more casual 'salon' is much more fun. Order the *dégustation* tapas-sized set menu (€79, with matching wines €99), where five courses arrive in matched pairs, each dish with descriptions longer than this review, but it's fantastic stuff.
☎ 01 42 22 00 11
🖥 darroze@relais chateaux.com ✉ 4 rue d'Assas, 6e 🕑 12.30-2.15pm & 7.30-10.15pm Tue-Sat 🅜 Sèvres-Babylone

Romantics, make a bee line for Le Petit Zinc

JEAN-BERNARD CARILLET

Polidor
(5, B3) $
French
You need to plan your visit to this intimate bistro to avoid an extended wait for a table. Arriving there on the dot of opening time can be tedious, but the combi-nation of atmosphere, traditional bistro fare and Victor Hugo–era prices make it a comforting experience.
☎ 01 43 26 95 34 ✉ 41 rue Monsieur-le-Prince, 6e 🕑 noon-2.30pm & 7pm-12.30am, to 11pm Sun 🅜 Odéon

When Smoke Gets In Your Eyes
So you've managed to squeeze into your bistro table with not inconsiderable effort after waiting for half an hour. Keeping your elbows in, you manage to peruse *la carte,* when your neighbouring tables simultaneously decide to light up stinky *Gitanes*. If you smoke, at least you know that you can light up after the meal, if you don't, welcome to Paris-style dining.

You could complain and be sent to that table next to the toilets or the swinging kitchen doors – the designated smoking area. You could sit outside, if the rain stopped. But you're probably going to sit and suffer, because while the law states that restaurants must have a nonsmoking area, the whole notion is treated with a disdain usually reserved for vegetarian meals and high-chair requests.

OBERKAMPF & BELLEVILLE

Astier
(3, J2) $$

While it's an unassuming, cheek-to-jowl bistro, some solid cooking, an interesting wine list and modest prices make this a welcoming experience. The service is friendly and knowledgeable, especially with wines – get them to recommend a *verre* (glass) to match your selection from the cheese basket, one of Paris' best.

☎ 01 43 57 16 35 ✉ 44 rue Jean-Pierre-Timbaud, 11e 🕑 noon-2pm & 8-11pm Ⓜ Parmentier

Dong Huong
(2, G3) $
Vietnamese

The best of the area's Asian food eateries, great bowls of *pho* (soup) are served to rooms full of hungry regulars, who are all Asian (mainly Vietnamese). This sign, plus the food coming out so fast is a testament to its authenticity. A real non-smoking section is a bonus.

☎ 01 43 57 18 88 ✉ 14 rue Louis-Bonnet, 11e 🕑 noon-11pm, Mon & Wed-Sun Ⓜ Belleville

Le Villaret
(3, J3) $$
Bistro

A mix of savvy locals and knowledgeable travelling foodies crowd into this simple bistro for the refined cooking of Olivier Gaslain. Order any of the classics, such as *sole meunière* leg of lamb or roasted chicken and it'll be memorable. There's an excellent wine list and the service is good-natured even when the place is full to the rafters.

☎ 01 43 57 89 76 ☎ 13 rue Ternaux, 11e 🕑 noon-2pm Mon-Fri & 8pm-midnight Mon-Sat Ⓜ Oberkampf

Le Vin du Zinc
(3, J3) $$
Bistro/Bar

This is the kind of eatery that every neighbourhood needs – with a blackboard menu that actually changes, plenty of interesting wines and flavoursome food that makes a great excuse to try another *vin*. The atmosphere is very relaxed.

☎ 01 48 06 28 23 ☎ 25 rue Oberkampf, 11e 🕑 noon-2pm & 8-11pm Tue-Sat Ⓜ Oberkampf

Le Zéphyr
(2, H2) $$
French

This elegant 1930s bistro is worth the trip for its refined cooking and genial ambience. A typical menu offers eggplant ravioli with mint vinaigrette and roasted lamb noisettes with anchovies and *crème brûlée à la tomate* to finish. Bookings advisable.

☎ 01 46 36 65 81 ✉ 1 rue du Jourdain, 20e 🕑 noon-2.30pm Mon-Fri & 8-11pm Mon-Sat Ⓜ Jourdain

Mon Vieil Ami knows how to make instant friends (p77)

JEAN-BERNARD CARILLET

ÎLE ST-LOUIS

Brasserie de l'Île St-Louis
(5, D3) $$
Alsatian
While not in the same
league as Brasserie Flo
(p72) or Brasserie Bofinger
(p64), the atmosphere
of this Alsatian brasserie
makes it a worthwhile
stop. Stuffed animal heads
glare down at you as you
tuck into *choucroute garnie*
(sauerkraut with prepared
meats) on communal
benches. Weather permit-
ting, the view of the Seine
from the terrace enhances
the standard fare.
☎ 01 43 54 02 59
✉ 55 quai de Bourbon,
4e ⏱ 11.30am-1am
Thu-Tue, from 6pm Thu
Ⓜ Pont Marie

Apéritif?
Alcoholic drinks are available wherever you eat, or at
cafés even if you don't eat. Many Parisians will start
with a glass of champagne (*une coupe*) or a beer (*une
pression*) as an apéritif, and then have wine with their
meal. Wine with meals generally starts at €15 a bottle,
with most being in the €20 to €30 range. It's always
good to check what locals are drinking – if everyone
is having house wine, follow suit. A selection of wines
is always available by the glass (*un verre*, €4–5) or jug
(*un pichet*, €6–10 depending on size).

Isami
(5, D3) $$
Japanese
This miniscule Japanese
restaurant stands well
ahead of the pack on the
Île St-Louis. It has created
its enviable reputation
through its practically
flapping fresh fish and less
common menu choices
such as sea urchin, as
well as *ika-natto* (sliced
raw squid overlaid with
fermented soybeans).
☎ 01 40 46 06 97
✉ 4 quai d'Orléans, 4e
⏱ noon-2pm Tue-Sat &
7-10pm Tue-Sun
Ⓜ Pont Marie

Mon Vieil Ami
(5, D3) $$$
Bistro
You're welcomed like an
old friend the minute you
arrive at this sleek black
bistro, and provided with
an apéritif of Alsatian pinot
blanc to sip while you pe-
ruse the interesting menu.
The pâté in pastry crust is a
fabulous starter and any of
the Alsatian casserole main
courses are worth exploring.
The chocolate tart is superb
and it's worth keeping in
mind that there is also a
daily lunch menu (€15).
☎ 01 40 46 01 35
✉ 69 St Louis en l'Île,
4e ⏱ noon-2.15pm &
8pm-10.15pm Wed-Sun
Ⓜ Pont Marie

Brasserie de l'Île St-Louis – a different sort of island fun

LATIN QUARTER

Fogon St-Julien

(5, C3) $$$

Spanish

This veteran eatery offers the most authentic Spanish cuisine in central Paris. The tapas is inventive, but it's definitely the cured meats and paella that really takes you south of the border. The *arroz Negro paella* (black rice with squid ink hiding chunks of fish, cuttlefish and shrimp) is superb.
☎ 01 43 54 31 33 ✉ 10 rue St-Julien-le-Pauvre, 5e 🕑 noon-2.30pm & 7pm-midnight Ⓜ Maubert-Mutualité

Le Jardin des Pâtes

(3, G6) $

Italian

The 'Garden of Pastas' has wholewheat, buckwheat, chestnut pasta made from 100% *biologique* (natural) stone-ground grains. There are several vegetarian dishes on the menu but it's not a vegetarian restaurant. The dishes are simple and filling.

Hearty menu at Le Petit Pontoise

Wine by the glass and excellent fresh organic juices are available. Book for dinner.
☎ 01 43 31 50 71 ✉ 4 rue Lacépède, 5e 🕑 noon-2.30pm & 7-11pm Tue-Sun Ⓜ Cardinal Lemoine Ⓥ

Le Petit Pontoise

(5, D3) $$

Bistro

This charming bistro features a blackboard menu full of seasonal delights. Standard dishes include the homemade foie gras accompanied with figs and *poulet fermier avec pommes purée* (roasted farm chicken with mashed potato) where the flavour absolutely transcends its simple ingredients.
☎ 01 43 29 25 20 ✉ 9 rue de Pontoise, 5e 🕑 noon-2pm & 7-10pm Ⓜ Maubert-Mutualité

Moissonnier knows how to leave big hints about the wine

Les Quatre et Une Saveurs
(3, G5) $$
Macrobiotic

This is one of Paris' few truly macrobiotic restaurants. The *assiette complète* (mixed plate) or the artistically presented *crudités* (white radishes pickled in plum vinegar, seaweed, beans, rice and millet) are good choices, as is the *mû* tea (made from 16 plants). There are tasty set *menus* at €13 (lunch) and €22/25 (dinner).
☎ 01 43 26 88 80 ✉ 72 rue du Cardinal Lemoine, 5e ⏲ noon-2.30pm & 7-10.30pm Tue-Sun Ⓜ Cardinal Lemoine Ⓥ

Moissonnier
(5, D4) $$$
Lyonnais

Whisper it when in Paris, but many believe that Lyon is France's gastronomic capital and this elegant eatery gives you a chance to sample the cuisine. The food is hearty fare, starting with the *quenelles* (fish dumplings), *boudin noir* (black pudding) and your best chance to try *tripe* as it should be done. The extensive dessert list also awaits.
☎ 01 43 29 87 65 ✉ 28 rue des Fossés St-Bernard, 5e ⏲ noon-1.30pm Tue-Sun & 7-9.30pm Tue-Sat Ⓜ Cardinal Lemoine

Restaurant du Hammam de la Mosquée
(3, H6) $
Moroccan

This multitasking mosque is a place of worship, a research centre, *hammam*, restaurant, and *salon de*

Food Markets

Paris' food markets are a sensory delight and are an experience not to be missed. For specialist food shops, see (p60).

- **Marché aux Enfants Rouges** (3, H3; rue de Bretagne, 3e; ⏲ 8am-1pm & 4-7.30pm Tue-Sat; Ⓜ Temple, Arts et Métiers) Excellent French and other European goodies.
- **Marché aux Puces d'Aligre** (2, G4; place d'Aligre, 12e; ⏲ 8am-1pm & 4-7.30pm Tue-Sat; Ⓜ Ledru Rollin) Has a colourful Arab and North African flavour.
- **Marché Belleville** (2, G3; blvd de Belleville, 11e; ⏲ 8am-1pm Tue & Fri; Ⓜ Belleville) Wonderful mix of African, Middle Eastern and Asian goods.
- **Marché Montorgueil** (3, G3; rue Montorgueil near rue de Tubigo, 1er; ⏲ 8am-7pm Tue-Sat, to noon Sun; Ⓜ Les Halles) Closest market to the much-missed Les Halles market.
- **Marché Mouffetard** (3, G6; rue Mouffetard near rue de l'Arbolète, 5e; ⏲ 8am-7pm Tue-Sat, to noon Sun; Ⓜ Censier Daubenton) Yes, it's a little touristy, but it sure is pretty.

Fresh-express rue Mouffetard

thé. You can combine these activities by taking the *formule orientale* (€58) that starts with being pummelled in the *hammam*, a 10-minute massage to help you forget the pummelling, followed by couscous with lamb or tagine and enough mint tea to float a boat.
☎ 01 43 31 38 20 ✉ 39 rue Geoffroy St-Hilaire, 5e ⏲ 12.30-3pm & 7.30-10.30pm Ⓜ Place Monge

TROCADÉRO & EIFFEL TOWER

Jules Verne
(3, A4) $$$$
Haute Cuisine
The food and service at this ageing all-black restaurant are no competition for the views from the window tables of this Eiffel Tower institution. Take someone you love, take the private elevator and take the (€51) lunch menu.
☎ 01 45 55 61 44
✉ 2nd level, Eiffel Tower, Champ de Mars, 7e
🕑 12.15-1.30pm & 7.15-9.30pm Ⓜ Bir-Hakeim

La Butte Chaillot
(3, A3) $$
Bistro
This fashionable eatery attracts suits for business lunches and affluent residents for dinner. The lamb fillet with basil and fennel is delicious. In a rare move, there are usually a couple of vegetarian dishes on offer.
☎ 01 47 27 88 88
✉ 110bis ave Kléber, 16e 🕑 noon-2.30pm Sun-Fri & 7pm-midnght Ⓜ Trocadéro Ⓥ

L'Astrance
(3, A4) $$$$
Contemporary
Several years after opening, Parisians still rave about eating here. At this exquisite split-level restaurant Chef Pascal Barbot has a deft touch and dishes like crab and avocado ravioli, lamb with eggplant and miso are classics. The short menu, small number of tables and excellent service offer a memorable experience. Book well ahead for dinner.

Coffee Lingo
un café A single shot of espresso.
une noisette A shot of espresso with a spot of milk.
un café crème A shot of espresso lengthened with steamed milk (closest thing to a caffè latte).
un café allongé An espresso lengthened with hot water (closest thing to American-style coffee).

GREG ELMS

Morning coffee with *tartin* – first flavours of the day

☎ 01 40 50 84 40 ✉ 4 rue Beethoven, 16e 🕑 12.30-2.30pm Wed-Sun & 8-11.30pm Tue-Sun Ⓜ Passy

Le Petit Rétro
(3, A2) $$
Bistro
From the gorgeous 'Petit Rétro' emblazoned on the *zinc* (bar), to the Art Nouveau tiles this is a handsome space. With a dish like *blanquette de veau* (a creamy veal stew) as one of the house specials, it's hearty, heart-warming stuff.
☎ 01 44 05 06 05
🖳 www.petitretro.fr ✉ 5 rue Mesnil, 16e 🕑 noon-2.30pm & 7-10.30pm Mon-Fri Ⓜ Victor Hugo

Passiflore
(3, A3) $$
Bistro
Chef Roland Durand spent years in Thailand and what he brings to the 'passion flower' is an eclectic mix of Indian and Thai spice notes and flavours using primarily French produce. The menu sometimes reads like fusion food gone awry – but a taste of any of the soups, for instance, removes any doubts. The service is assured and there is an excellent wine list.
☎ 01 47 04 96 81 ✉ 33 rue de Longchamp, 16e 🕑 noon-2pm & 7.30-10.30pm Mon-Fri, 8-10.30pm Sat Ⓜ Trocadéro

Entertainment

Paris offers myriad entertainment opportunities including classical musical recitals, often in local churches, hip-hop gigs, ballets and some of the best avant-garde dance you'll see anywhere. While Paris has always excelled at delivering capital Culture with a capital 'C', it's only in the last few years that it's figured out how to really relax and partake in the simple pleasure of a happy hour.

This doesn't mean that Paris is going into a cultural nosedive – try getting tickets for an opera or strike up a conversation about which smoky little jazz club is better. Parisians have always loved film and you find them lined up to buy tickets whenever any new film gets some positive press. Parisian theatre is also well attended and is wonderfully eclectic, but you'll need good French to appreciate it, except when one of the frequent international tours is in town. Overseas acts are always on as Parisians love discovering something fresh. Musically you can catch acts as diverse as North African jazz troupes and Indian tabla and sitar recitals – often on the one bill. Touring rock bands from stadium acts to indie label stalwarts make a point of booking gigs in Paris and you might find it easier to get tickets here than at home.

New hip little bars seem to be popping up all over Paris and while the clubs are no match for other major world capitals like London, there's enough diversity to suit every taste.

Listings & Bookings

To check what's on in Paris proceed directly to a newsstand and purchase *Pariscope*, *L'Officiel des Spectacles*, or **Zurban** (www.zurban.com in French), all of which come out on Wednesday. For up-to-date information on clubs and the music scene, pick up a free copy of *LYLO* (short for *les yeux, les oreilles*, meaning 'ears and eyes') with listings of live music. The monthly magazine **Nova** (www.novaplanet.com) has good clubbing information.

Reservations are recommended for all performances. You can buy tickets for most cultural events at several outlets, the most convenient being **FNAC** (p50) and **Virgin Megastore** (p59).

Kiosque Théâtre (3, C7; 15 place de la Madeleine, 9e; 12.30-7.45pm Tue-Sat, to 3.45pm Sun; M Madeleine) sells half-price tickets (plus €2.45 commission) for same-day performances. There's another branch in front of **Gare Montparnasse** (2, E5) with the same opening hours.

Blow your mind at FNAC Musique

Special Events

January/February *La Grande Parade de Paris* (www.parisparade.com) – New Year's Day celebration with concerts and events before the big parade, see the website for details as the event is mobile.

Chinese New Year – the ubiquitous dragon parades are held in Chinatown (13e) and rue Au Maire (3e).

March/April *Banlieues Bleues* (www.banlieuesbleues.org) – this jazz and blues festival throws world, soul and funk music into the mix at its festival held in St-Denis.

April *Marathon International de Paris* (www.parismarathon.com) – midmonth; from place de la Concorde (1er) to av Foch (16e) and includes a half marathon.

May/June *Internationaux de France de Tennis* (French Open Tennis Tournament; www.frenchopen.com) – takes places in Stade Roland Garros; it's a Grand Slam tournament.

June *Gay Pride* (www.gaypride.fr, in French) – late June; a colourful Saturday afternoon parade through the Marais.

Fête de la Musique (www.fetedelamusique.culture.fr) – 21 June; featuring impromptu live performances.

June/July *La Course des Garçons de Café* – hundreds of waiters and waitresses race through central Paris carrying a glass and a bottle balanced on a tray (it's the fastest you'll ever see a waiter move in Paris).

July *La Goutte d'Or en Fête* (www.gouttedorenfete.org) – world music festival featuring raï, reggae and rap among other music styles, which happens at place de Léon, 18e.

Bastille Day – 14 July; France's national day is best spent in Paris, with *bals des sapeurs-pompiers* (dances sponsored by Paris' firefighters) held at fire stations (on the night of the 13th); a fire brigade and military parade travels along the av des Champs Élysées (10am); a huge display of *feux d'artifice* (fireworks) either near the Eiffel Tower or at the Invalides (around 11pm).

Tour de France (www.letour.fr) – 3rd or 4th Sun; the world's most prestigious cycling event ends on the av des Champs Élysées.

Paris Plage (www.paris.fr) – Paris' own *plage* has been an amazing success with 3km of faux-Biarritz beaches starting at quai Henry IV (1er) and ending at the quai des Tuileries (4e).

September *Jazz à la Villette* (www.cite-musique.fr) – early in the month; 10-day jazz festival with sessions predominately held in Parc de la Villette, at the Cité de la Musique.

Festival d'Automne (www.festival-automne.com) – commences September; Autumn festival of music and theatre with performances held throughout the city over three months.

October *Foire Internationale d'Art Contemporain* (*FIAC*; www.fiac-online.com) – huge contemporary art fair with some 150 galleries represented.

December *Christmas Eve Mass* – 24–25 December; midnight Mass is celebrated at many Paris churches, including Notre Dame (get there before 11pm).

New Year's Eve – 31 December; festivities take place on blvd St-Michel (5e), Eiffel Tower (7e) and av des Champs Élysées (8e).

PUBS, BARS & CAFÉS

Andy Wahloo (3, G3)
Brought to you by same people as Momo (London) and 404 (next door, p70), Andy Wahloo is one of Paris' hippest drinking spots. Arrive early evening to check out the funky Moroccan décor. You can try *shisha* pipes, you must try a cocktail and you can order some alcohol-soaking food from next door.
☎ 01 42 71 20 38 ✉ 69 rue des Gravilliers, 3e ⏲ noon-2am, Mon-Sat Ⓜ Arts et Métiers

Buddha Bar (3, D2) If the enormous bronze Buddha (this legendary cavernous restaurant/bar centrepiece) could talk, he'd probably say that he preferred the old days when former DJ Claude Challe's sets sounded fresh, the crowd was uniformly beautiful, the camera flashes were from paparazzi rather than gawking tour

groups and there wasn't a gift shop. If you haven't been before, go for a cocktail and try to wipe the tear from the Buddha's eye.
☎ 01 53 05 90 00 ✉ 8 rue Boissy d'Anglas, 8e ⏲ 6pm-2am Ⓜ Concorde

Café Beaubourg (5, C1)
The main attraction of this Hôtel Costes (p97) café is the great Centre Pompidou views from the terrace, where you can debate the merits of the Pompidou's inside-out architecture. Skip the food and enjoy a drink and what passes for entertainment on the square.
☎ 01 48 87 63 96 ✉ 100 rue St-Martin, 1er ⏲ 8am-1am Mon-Fri, 8am-2am Sat & Sun Ⓜ Chatelet-Les Halles

Café Charbon (2, G3) A perennial Parisian favourite, this was the prototype for

Oberkampf's hip cafés – and it's still the best. You can drop in for decent coffee in the morning, meet friends for a casual snack later in the day or make a night of it when Nouveau Casino (p87), opens next door.
☎ 01 43 57 55 13 ✉ 109 rue Oberkampf, 11e ⏲ 9am-2am Ⓜ Parmentier

Café de Flore (5, A2) Café de Flore is best visited in the late afternoon when the likes of Sartre, de Beauvoir, Camus and Picasso took time out to imbibe at this lovely Art Deco café. Sit on the terrace and sip a beer, but if there are no spare tables, head over to **Les Deux Magots** (5, A2, opposite) for a similar trip back in time.
☎ 01 45 48 55 26 ✉ 172 blvd St-Germain, 6e ⏲ 7.30-1.30am Ⓜ St-Germain des Prés

Make wine-drinking your business at Café de l'Industrie (p84)

JEAN-BERNARD CARILLET

Café de l'Industrie (5, F2)
Having proved such a success in its initial location this café and restaurant has taken over the café across the road. Powerbook-wielding writers and groups of students pretending to work dominate the eclectic furniture between meals, and the place gets buzzy late at night.
☎ 01 47 00 13 53
✉ 16/17 rue St-Sabin, 11e ⏰ 10am-2am
Ⓜ Bastille

Chai 33 (2, H5) Yet another Thierry Bégué (Buddha Bar et al) project, this former storehouse has transformed into a fantastic venue for wine lovers, with a restaurant, lounge, tasting room and shop. Wine has been divided into six groups and colour-coded for flavour and depth instead of variety: red is 'fruity and intense', green

is 'light and spirited', etc. In Paris that equals anarchy.
☎ 01 53 44 01 01 ✉ 33 cour St-Émilion, 12e
⏰ noon-2am Ⓜ Cour St-Émilion

Chez Prune (3, J2) In this neighbourhood where pram-pushing metrosexuals meet for a chat, its residents probably collectively willed Chez Prune into existence. The café has that great local vibe and is packed for lunch, while later on the decent snacks are good and *mojitos* are the drink of choice.
☎ 01 42 41 30 47
✉ 71 quai de Valmy, 10e ⏰ 8am-2am Mon-Sat, 10am-2am Sun
Ⓜ République

China Club (3, J5) A seductive and stylish establishment, the endless bar, high ceilings and low lighting make this a *très*

alluring space. Decked out in the style of a far-Eastern faux-gentleman's club, it has a *fumoir* (smoking room) on the 1st floor and a jazz club in the basement. The bar is the ultimate place – a couple of their martinis really kick off the night in style.
☎ 01 43 43 82 02 ✉ 50 rue de Charenton, 12e
⏰ 7pm-2am, happy hour 7-9pm Ⓜ Ledru Rollin

Fu Bar (5, B3) Sure you'll hear English being yelled over the top of the eclectic music played in this tiny two-storey bar, but the mix of clientele includes enough Parisians to make you not feel too guilty. Delicious cocktails and strong spirits keep the conversation flowing and the place packed.
☎ 01 40 51 82 00
✉ 5 rue St-Sulpice, 6e
⏰ 5pm-2am Ⓜ Odéon

Le Clown Bar knows how to put on a happy face (p85)

Harry's New York Bar
(3, E2) Loved more by expats than Parisians, fans of the Bloody Mary won't want to miss the alleged home of its creation. It's surprisingly (and welcomingly) scruffy and the waiters, reassuringly bedecked in white coats, mix some of Paris' most treacherous cocktails. Drink with caution or you'll find yourself ending the night in the downstairs piano bar.
☎ 01 42 61 71 14
✉ 5 rue Daunou, 2e
🕓 10.30am-4am Mon-Sat M Opéra

L'Apparement Café
(5, E1) A cosy home away from home, this charming café makes a great stop after a Musée Picasso visit. With its wood panelling, leather sofas, parlour games and dog-eared books, it's the kind of place to settle in for a couple of hours. There's a decent brunch on Sunday's until 4pm.
☎ 01 48 87 12 22 ✉ 18 rue des Coutures St-Germain, 3e 🕓 noon-2am Mon-Fri, 4pm-2am Sat, 12.30pm-midnight Sun M St-Sébastien Froissart

Le Bar du Plaza-Athénée
(3, B2) The gorgeous iceberg blue bar, constructed of glass and beautifully backlit, visually enchants this stunning bar. Cocktail in hand, you can either admire the bar at close quarters or sit back in a leather armchair and watch the high-wattage clientele try to match the star power of the bar.
☎ 01 53 67 65 00
✉ Hôtel Plaza Athénée,

So cool, it's icy – Le Bar du Plaza Athénée

JEAN-BERNARD CARILLET

25 av de Montaigne, 8e
🕓 6pm-2am
M Alma-Marceau

Le Clown Bar (3, J3) Just a couple of clown shoe-sized steps from the Cirque d'Hiver (Winter Circus), this wine bar resembles a museum of circus memorabilia. There are decent wines by the glass and the food on offer is traditional and hearty, but coulrophobia sufferers – and you know who you are – should give this place a wide berth because sinister clown images abound.
☎ 01 43 55 87 35
✉ 114 rue Amelot, 11e
🕓 noon-3pm & 7.30pm-1am Mon-Sat, 7pm-1am Sun M Filles du Calvaire

Le Fumoir (5, B1) An attractive space for a similarly aesthetically pleasing crowd who sip martinis at the bar and pretend to read in the library. Friendlier than you'd expect, it's the perfect place to put your feet up and get into some some people-watching after a picture-watching session at the nearby Louvre. The service is excellent; the barmen know their cocktails

and the food is appetising as well.
☎ 01 42 92 00 24 ✉ 6 rue de l'Amiral Coligny, 1er 🕓 11am-2am
M Louvre-Rivoli ♿ OK

Le Lèche-Vin (5, F2)
There's nothing quite like this bar-cum-shrine to the Virgin Mary in the Bastille. Taking in this redefinition of religious kitsch while having a drink is a unique experience, but those who see little humour in sacrilegious displays of religious iconography had better not head to the toilets.
☎ 01 43 55 98 91 ✉ 13 rue Duval, 11e 🕓 7pm-2am Mon-Sat, 7pm-midnight Sun M Bastille

SanzSans (5, F3) A must-do on any Bastille bar hop, the young crowd turn this bar with red velvet Gothic décor into something wild by midnight. It does serve decent food, but it's best to come for the DJ and drinks. Music can be anything from hip-hip to soul and funk.
☎ 01 44 75 78 78
🖥 www.sanzsans.com
✉ 49 rue du Faubourg St-Antoine, 11e
🕓 9am-2am M Bastille

DANCE CLUBS

Batofar (2, G5) Only Parisians could make a club set in an Irish lighthouse-boat (moored on the Seine) cool. The club has set a new course recently; Mondays are jazz, Wednesday's live music, Thursday's dub/reggae and the weekends focus on dance and house, with great DJs.

☎ 01 56 29 10 00
🖥 www.batofar.org
✉ opp 11 quai Françoise Mauriac, 13e € free-€12 🕐 9pm-midnight Mon & Tue, to 4am, 5am or 6am Wed-Sun Ⓜ Bibliothèque François Mitterand

Folies Pigalle (4, C3) Famous for its after parties and theme nights, this party place attracts a mixed gay and straight crowd depending on the night (or day!). With a versatile roster of resident and guest DJs, popular events are Heavenly and the Breakfast Klub after party held on Wednesdays.

☎ 01 48 78 55 25

🖥 www.folies-pigalle .com ✉ 11 place Pigalle, 9e € free-€20 🕐 midnight-dawn Tue-Sat, 7pm-midnight Sun Ⓜ Pigalle

La Loco (4, B3) One of Paris' perennially popular mainstream clubs, La Loco (formerly Locomotive), fills its floors with Paris' young suburban clubbers out for a good time. Music ranges from techno, groove and disco and rock across its three levels.

☎ 01 53 41 88 88
🖥 www.laloco.com
✉ 90 blvd de Clichy, 18e € €9-16 🕐 11pm-6am (Sat & Sun to 7am, Mon from midnight) Ⓜ Blanche

Le Manray (3, C2) We wouldn't make a detour here for sushi, but once the wasabi gets cleared away celebrities and those that resemble them jump on to the dancefloor. Those who hate waiting in line can arrive early and eat,

those in the know skip the line and pretend they know the celebrity owners: Johnny Depp, Sean Penn, John Malkovich and Mick Hucknall.

☎ 01 56 88 36 36 34
🖥 www.manray.fr
✉ 32-34 rue Marbeuf, 8e € free Mon-Thu, Sun, €20 after 12.30am Fri, Sat 🕐 6pm-2am Mon-Thu, 6pm-5am Fri & Sat, 7pm-2am Sun Ⓜ Franklin D Roosevelt

Le Triptyque (3, F2) While still running what seems an impossibly eclectic programme from French *chansons* (see p90) to indie pop and electro to hip-hop and soul/funk, this recently opened club always has something interesting happening. Check the website for programming details.

☎ 01 40 28 05 45
🖥 www.letriptyque .com ✉ 142 rue Montmartre, 2e € free-€13 🕐 8.30pm-6am Tue-Sun Ⓜ Grands Boulevards

Le Wax (5, F2) It's worth getting to this bar/club early to check out the 'retro-futuristic' décor, settle into a lounge or one of the groovy chairs and order a lethal cocktail. During the week DJs spin funk and disco, while on the weekends its house and electro – generally with funky house pumping until dawn.

☎ 01 40 21 16 16
🖥 www.le-wax.com
✉ 15 rue Daval, 11e € free 🕐 6pm-2am

ROB FLYNN

Not having a blast at Batofor means mutiny

Tue-Thu, 6pm-5am Fri & Sat, happy hour 6-9pm Ⓜ Bastille

Les Bains (3, G3) While the in-crowd are less obvious at this former *hammam,* the celebrities still flock here and the bouncers make it a trial for the average punter to get in. However, Wednesday nights, featuring garage/house, are worthwhile – just dress and approach with attitude. ☎ 01 48 87 01 80 ✉ 7 rue du Bourg-l'Abbé, 3e Ⓔ €16-20 ⊙ 11.30pm-5am Mon-Sat Ⓜ Étienne Marcel

Nirvana (3, C2) Claude Challe, the original Buddha Bar (p83) DJ and soundtrack provider for a million Eastern-themed, candle-lit, dinner parties, opened this club/restaurant in 2002. Nights here can vary wildly, but the cocktails are excellent and if you've enjoyed Challe's compilations, you'll probably make a beeline for it anyway. ☎ 01 53 89 18 91 ✉ 3 av Matignon, 8e Ⓔ free ⊙ 8am-4am Ⓜ Franklin D Roosevelt

Nouveau Casino (2, G3) This extension of popular Café Charbon (p83), has become one of Paris' best venues not only for live music but its club nights as well. Guest DJs such as Bertrand Burgalat fit into the calendar alongside popular club night Minimal Dancing and indie rock acts. ☎ 01 43 57 57 40 ⌨ www.nouveaucasino .net in French ✉ 109

Jiving to the groove at Nouveau Casino is a sure bet

JEAN-BERNARD CARILLET

rue Oberkampf, 11e Ⓔ free-€18 ⊙ 9pm or 11pm-2am or 5am Ⓜ Parmentier

Rex Club (3, G2) When the Rex celebrated its 15th birthday, Laurent Garnier, the superstar DJ who enshrined his name here, played a mammoth 12-hour set. And just like

Garnier, this club is still pumping strongly; the house nights (Thursday and Saturday) are definitely the best in town as is Friday's Automatik (techno). ☎ 01 42 36 10 96 ✉ 5 blvd Poissonière, 2e Ⓔ free-€16 ⊙ Wed-Sat 11pm-dawn Ⓜ Bonne Nouvelle

Flying Solo

If you're on your own in Paris it can be a little difficult to meet people, especially Parisians, if you don't speak French. Here are a few places where it shouldn't be too hard to strike up a conversation.

- **Fu Bar** (p84) A friendly bar that's so crowded you can't help but make friends.
- **L'Atelier de Joël Robuchon** (p74) The bench style eating might have upset this chef's fans, but it's great for solo diners.
- **Pari Roller Ramble** (p37) When there are several thousand people who you already have something in common with (those inline skates on your feet!) you can't help but make friends.
- **Shakespeare and Co** (p57) We know it's a bookshop and you're supposed to be quiet, but it's a great place to meet people.

CINEMAS

Pariscope and *L'Officiel des Spectacles* list the cinematic offerings alphabetically by their French title followed by the English (or German, Italian, Spanish etc) one. If a movie is labelled 'vo' (for *version originale*) it means it will be subtitled rather than dubbed ('vf' or *version Française*), so 'vo' Hollywood movies will still be in English. A selection of cinemas showing more interesting films is listed here.

Hi-tech Cinémathèque

Cinéma des Cinéastes (4, A3) This three-screen cinema is dedicated to quality cinema, whether French, foreign or avant-garde. Thematic seasons, documentaries and meet-the-director sessions round out the programme. ☎ 01 53 42 40 20 ✉ 7 av de Clichy Ⓜ Place de Clichy ♿ OK

Cinémathèque Française (2, H5) This government-supported cultural institution almost always leaves its foreign offerings – often seldom-screened classics – in the original, nondubbed version. At the time of writing it was in the process of relocating to a new address (shown below). Screenings were set to recommence in late 2005. ☎ 01 53 65 74 74 🖥 www.cinematheque francaise.com ✉ 51 rue de Bercy Ⓜ Cour St-Émilion

Forum des Images (5, C1) This archive cinema beneath the sprawling Forum des Halles is a film buff's idea of heaven, with rarely screened and little known films on the programme. There are usually between four and five screenings each day. ☎ 01 44 76 62 00 🖥 www.forumdes images.net in French ✉ 1 Grande Galerie, Porte St-Eustache, Forum des Halles, 1er ⏰ 1-10pm Tue, 1-9pm Wed-Sun Ⓜ Les Halles

Taking Thé

Taking tea is a ritual for many travellers to Paris and tea is making quite a comeback in the capital. Here are a couple of favourite places to sit back, relax and sip a brew.

- **A Priori Thé** (3, F2; ☎ 01 42 97 48 75; 35-37 galerie Vivienne, 2e; ⏰ 3-6pm Mon-Fri; Ⓜ Bourse) Located in the glorious Galerie Vivienne, this tearoom serves up excellent brews and hearty cakes. There are great people-watching opportunities from the tables outside and a no-nonsense weekend brunch (9am-6.30pm Sat, noon-6.30pm Sun).
- **Angelina** (3, E2; ☎ 01 42 60 82 00; 226 rue de Rivoli, 1er; ⏰ 9.45am-6.45pm; Ⓜ Tuileries) This historic tearoom is where Louvre-weary tourists line up to taste the tea and terrific meringue and the locals imbibe the glorious hot chocolate.
- **Ladurée** (3, B2; ☎ 01 40 75 08 75; 75 av des Champs Élysées, 8e; ⏰ 8.30am-7pm; Ⓜ George V) This sumptuous *belle époque* tearoom, running since 1862, is a Parisian institution and has legendary pastries. Specialities are *macarons au chocolat* (chocolate macaroons) and *macarons à la pistache* (pistachio macaroons).

ROCK, JAZZ & FRENCH CHANSONS

The most popular venues for medium to large international acts include Le Zénith (p90), the Palais Omnisports de Paris-Bercy (p95), l'Olympia (p95) and the Stade de France (p95). Expect to pay from €20 to €50.

Au Lapin Agile (4, D1)
This rustic Montmartre institution was a favourite haunt of artists and intellectuals at the turn of the 20th century. These days, *chansons* (see p90) and poetry readings are performed in front of die-hard locals and expectant tourists. There's still old-time Montmartre magic in the air on a good night.
☎ 01 46 06 85 87
🖥 www.au-lapin-agile
.com ✉ 22 rue des Saules, 18e € €24/17 (includes one free drink)
🕐 9pm-2am Tue-Sun
Ⓜ Lamarck Caulaincourt

Café de la Danse (5, F2)
This venue offers up a wide variety of acts from *oud* (Arabic lute) playing jazz quartets to US indie acts. Traditional French *chansons*

and dance are on the roster as well and it's a reasonably intimate (300–500 seats) venue to see some great performers.
☎ 01 47 00 57 59
🖥 www.cafédeladanse
.com in French ✉ 5 passage Louis-Philippe, 11e € €10-20 🕐 box office noon-6pm Mon-Fri
Ⓜ Bastille ♿ OK

La Cigale/La Boule Noir (4, D3) This elegantly faded music hall is a great midsized venue for visiting indie, rock and punk acts, as well as local favourites, especially Goth and metal bands (whose fans are hardcore). The balcony seats are excellent while down the front it's fun or dangerous – depending on who's playing.
☎ 01 49 25 89 99
🖥 www.lacigale.fr

✉ 102 blvd Rochech-ouart, 18e Ⓜ Pigalle

Le Baiser Salé (5, C1) The 'Salty Kiss' has a *salle de jazz* (jazz room) on the 1st floor with concerts of pop/rock and *chansons* at 7pm and Afro-jazz and jazz fusion at 10pm. There's a free jam session on Monday night.
☎ 01 42 33 37 71 ✉ 58 rue des Lombards, 1er
€ free-€20 🕐 bar 6pm-6am; salle de jazz 10pm-3am Ⓜ Châtelet

Le Bataclan (5, J3) Built in 1864, this enchanting concert hall draws French acts plus a diverse range of international acts from Moloko to Metallica. Check out the wonderful Bataclan Café while you're there.
☎ 01 43 14 35 35
✉ 50 blvd Voltaire, 11e

Close up and personal at Le Limonaire

€ €15-50 ☉ 8pm-late;
box office 11am-7pm
Mon-Sat Ⓜ Oberkampf
♿ OK

Le Caveau de la
Huchette (5, C3) This
medieval *cave* (cellar) was
utilised as a torture chamber during the Revolution;
however, these days it's
better known as a jazz
venue with a wonderful
post-WWII legacy. While
plenty come along to check
out the room, when there's
a good act on the place
still cooks.
☎ 01 43 26 65 05
🖳 www.caveaudela
huchette.fr ✉ 5 rue de la
Huchette, 5e € Mon-Thu
€10.50, Fri & Sat €13/9
☉ 9.30pm-2.30am,
to 3.30am, to 4am Sat
Ⓜ St-Michel

Le Divan du Monde
(4, C3) Great sightlines and
crisp sound have given this
venue an enviable reputa-
tion. These days it plays
host to an eclectic mix

of music including world
music and hip-hop along-
side indie/rock acts. It's
also a popular dance club,
with most nights kicking on
until 5am.
☎ 01 40 05 06 99
🖳 www.divandumonde
.com ✉ 75 rue des
Martyrs, 18e € free-
€20 ☉ from 7.30pm
Mon-Sat, from 2pm Sun
Ⓜ Pigalle

Le Limonaire (3, G2)
This intimate wine bar is
the most reliable place to
listen to traditional French
chansons in Paris. But come
here only if you're inter-
ested in the genreleft –
bar talk immediately
ceases when the perform-
ers take to the stage.
☎ 01 45 23 33 33
🖳 http://limonaire
.free.fr/in French
✉ 18 cité Bergère, 9e
€ free ☉ 6pm-mid-
night Tue-Sun; perform-
ances 10pm Tue-Sat,
7pm Sun Ⓜ Grands
Boulevards

Le Zénith (2, H1)
Barely a seat with an inter-
rupted view of the stage
in the house and excellent
acoustics make this one
of Paris' favourite venues.
Expect to see international
acts across the spectrum,
such as Green Day and Kylie,
take the stage – thankfully
not on the same night.
☎ 01 42 08 60 00
🖳 www.le-zenith.com
(in French) ✉ 211 av
Jean Jaurès, 19e
Ⓜ Porte de Pantin

L'Olympia (3, E2)
The Olympia has hosted
some big names in
entertainment over the
years – some of them still
coming back – such as
Chuck Berry and Engelbert
Humperdinck. But its not
all acts from your parents
(or grandparents) record
collection, acts like Good
Charlotte and Keane play
here as well.
☎ 08 92 68 33 68
🖳 www.olympiahall.
com ✉ 28 blvd des
Capucines, 9e ☉ box
office noon-7pm Mon-Fri
Ⓜ Opéra

New Morning (3, G1)
New Morning is a respected
venue hosting jazz and
a diverse range of world
music three to seven nights
a week at 9pm, with the
second set ending at
about 1am.
☎ 01 45 23 51 41
🖳 www.newmorning
.com in French ✉ 7-9
rue des Petites Écuries,
10e € €14.50-21
☉ 8pm-2am, box office
4.30-7.30pm Mon-Fri
Ⓜ Château d'Eau

Chansons
While *chanson* literally means 'song' in French, if you
say you're going to see *chanson,* this refers to a style
of music that combines a song of simple character,
with a melodramatic presentation. The French singers that defined *chanson* through the 20th century
were Édith Piaf, Maurice Chevalier and the infamous
Serge Gainsbourg. You'll probably see acts working
in the same style as these luminaries, accompanied
by a piano or accordion. New bands update the genre
and it's worth seeking out live performances (and
CDs) by bands such as Java (🖳 www.javasite.net),
who combine beats with classic *chanson* sounds and
Paris Combo (🖳 www.pariscombo.com) with the
enigmatic vocals of Belle du Berry.

THEATRE & COMEDY

Almost all of Paris' theatre productions are performed in French. There are a few English-speaking troupes, though. Look for ads on metro poster boards.

Café de la Gare (5, D1)
The 'Station Café' is one of the longest-running café/theatres in Paris, with comic theatre and stand-up acts that you'll need good French to understand.
☎ 01 42 78 52 51
🖥 www.café-de-la-gare .fr.st in French ✉ 41 rue du Temple, 4e € €16-19/8-16 🕐 Wed-Sat 8 & 10pm Ⓜ Hôtel de Ville

**Comédie Française
(3, F3)** Comédie Française is the world's oldest national theatre (founded in 1680 under Louis XIV), with a repertoire covering works of French luminaries. In recent years modern and even non-French works have been staged in its three theatres.
☎ 01 44 58 15 15
🖥 www.comedie

JEAN-BERNARD CARILLET

Arty Comédie Française

-francaise.fr ✉ 2 rue de Richelieu, 1er € €5-32 🕐 box office 11am-6pm Ⓜ Palais Royal

Hôtel du Nord (3, J1) The 'Hotel of the North' is the main venue for English-language stand-up comedians presented by Laughing Matters – who also bring an impressive roster of acoustic-based musicians to Paris.
Laughing Matters ☎ 01 53 19 98 88 🖥 www. anythingmatters.com ✉ 102 quai de Jemmapes, 10e € €20-22 Ⓜ République

Odéon Théâtre de l'Europe (5, B3) This huge, ornate 1780s theatre stages French classics, contemporary plays and works in their original languages (subtitled in French) plus theatre troupes from abroad. At the time of writing the Odéon was undergoing renovation (until late 2005) and plays are staged at the **Ateliers Berthier** (2, D1; ☎ 01 44 85 40 40; ✉ 8 blvd Berthier, 17e; € €13-26; 🕐 box office 11am-6.30pm Mon-Sat; Ⓜ Porte de Clichy).
☎ 01 44 41 36 36 🖥 www.theatre-odeon .fr ✉ 1 place Paul Claudel, 6e Ⓜ Odéon

Point Virgule (5, D2)
A vibrant atmosphere entices the punters towards this popular Marais spot,

with an encouraging crowd out for a good time and prepared to give new comedy and musical performances a fair hearing.
☎ 01 42 78 67 03 ✉ 7 rue Ste-Croix de la Bretonnerie, 4e € €15/12 🕐 shows 7.30pm, 9pm & 10pm Ⓜ Hôtel de Ville

**Théâtre de la Ville – Salle des Abbesses
(4, C2)** This red-and-cream neoclassical building in Montmartre mainly stages the contemporary dramatic productions of the Théâtre de la Ville (p93), as well as music and dance.
☎ 01 42 74 22 77 🖥 www.theatre delaville-paris.com ✉ 31 rue des Abbesses, 18e € €15-30 🕐 box office Tue-Sat 5-8pm Ⓜ Abbesses

Théâtre des Bouffes du Nord (2, F2) The beautifully 'distressed' décor of this theatre is a reminder of the adventurous joint programming of Peter Brook and Stéphane Lissner. Contemporary opera, classical and jazz music are all performed here. Experimental theatre takes the stage as well.
☎ 01 46 07 34 50 🖥 www.bouffesdu nord.com ✉ 37bis blvd de la Chapelle, 10e € €12-18.50 🕐 box office 11am-6pm Mon-Sat Ⓜ La Chapelle

CLASSICAL MUSIC, OPERA & DANCE

Cité de la Musique (2, H1) The 'City of Music' at the Parc de la Villette (p25) hosts a wide-ranging, interesting programme of music and dance in its 1200-seat auditorium. There's also a conservatorium and a small amphitheatre that's part of the museum where instruments from the collection are often played. ☎ 01 44 84 44 84 🖥 www.cite-musique .fr ✉ 221 av Jean Jaurès, 19e € €6-34 ☺ box office noon-6pm Tue-Sun Ⓜ Porte de Pantin ♿ OK

Châtelet-Théâtre Musical de Paris (5, C2) This lovely hall hosts operas, concerts (including some by the excellent Orchestre de Paris) and theatre performances. Classical music is also per-

Palais Garnier (p93) has the Midas touch

formed at 11am on Sunday (€20) and at 12.45pm on Monday, Wednesday and Friday (€9).
☎ 01 40 28 28 40 for reservations 🖥 www .chatelet-theatre.com in French ✉ 1 place du Châtelet, 1er € €8-106 ☺ box office Mon-Sat 11am-7pm Ⓜ Châtelet ♿ OK

Le Regard du Cygne (2, H2) The 'Look of the Swan' is a magnet for Paris' innovative talents in movement, music and theatre. This performance space features creative, often daring, modern dance in a great space.
☎ 01 43 58 55 93 ✉ 210 rue de Belleville, 20e € €15 Ⓜ Place des Fîtes

Opéra Bastille (5, F3) The Opéra National de Paris (ONP) performs here and the Palais Garnier, its old home. The Opéra Bastille opened in 1989 and, like the Palais Garnier, also stages ballets and concerts put on by the Opéra National's affiliated orchestra, choir and ballet companies. The opera season lasts from September to July.
☎ 08 92 69 78 68 🖥 www.opera-de-paris .fr ✉ 2-6 place de la Bastille, 12e € ballet/ chamber music/opera €70/16/114; book online, or by mail (Opéra National de Paris, 120 rue de

Can-Do Cancan

Perhaps we should thank a couple of Aussies for renewing interest in these risqué cabaret revues that everyone assumed had long decamped (and we mean 'camp') to Las Vegas. Baz Luhrmann's 2001 film, *Moulin Rouge* starring fellow Australian Nicole Kidman, has tourists taking in shows at the **Moulin Rouge** (4, B3 ☎ 01 53 09 82 82 🖥 www .moulinrouge.fr ✉ 82 blvd de Clichy, 18e € dinner & show €135/150/165, 9pm & 11pm shows €95/85; Ⓜ Blanche) rather than just treating the place as a photo opportunity on the Montmartre tourist trail.

While there are other cabaret revues in town, if you're going to go to one it's pretty hard to go past the most famous. The dinner and show package starts at 7pm and includes the 9pm show. You can also just take just the show at 9pm or 11pm. All three include a half bottle of champagne in the price.

Lyon, 75576 Paris Cedex 12)/phone/box office 10/4/2wks ahead ☾ box office 11am-6.30pm Mon-Sat Ⓜ Bastille

Opéra Comique (3, F2)
The 'Comic Opera' is a century-old hall that premiered numerous important French operas. It continues to present classic and lesser-known operas thanks to its director, Jérôme Savary. The season lasts from late October to early July.
☎ 08 25 00 00 58 for reservations 🖥 www .opera-comique.com ✉ 5 rue Favart, 2e € €7-170; tickets (limited visibility) up to 12hr before curtain €10 ; discounts 15mins before curtain for students, youth & seniors ☾ box office (opp 14 rue Favart) 9am-9pm Mon-Sat, 11am-7pm Sun Ⓜ Richelieu Drouot & OK

Palais Garnier (3, E2)
The extravagant Palais Garnier is the traditional home of the Opéra National de Paris (see also Opéra Bastille, opposite) and it remains better loved by Parisians. While most of the major opera performances are now held at Bastille, the Palais Garnier offers outstanding acoustics, though not all seats have great views.
☎ 08 92 69 78 68 🖥 www.opera-de-paris .fr ✉ place de l'Opéra, 9e € €7-64 ballet, €7-105 opera; tickets on sale 2wks prior to performances; booking details as per Opéra Bastille ☾ box office 11am-6.30pm Mon-Sat Ⓜ Opéra & OK

Théâtre de la Ville (4, C2)
Avant-garde dance, theatre and music is the attraction of this amphitheatre. The music programme features performances as

diverse as Iranian classical chants and sitar recitals.
☎ 01 42 74 22 77 🖥 www.theatre delaville-paris.com (in French) ✉ 2 place du Châtelet, 4e € €15-25 ☾ box office 11am-7pm Mon, 11am-8pm Tue-Sat Ⓜ Châtelet & OK

Théâtre des Champs Élysées (3, B2) This magnificent Right Bank orchestral and recital hall, was infamous as the venue where Stravinsky debuted his *Le Sacre du Printemps* (The Rite of Spring) in 1913, to a rather hostile response. These days it's a little tamer, offering a wide-ranging programme including jazz as well as voice recitals.
☎ 01 49 52 50 50 🖥 www.theatrechamps elysees.fr ✉ 15 av Montaigne, 8e € €110 ☾ box office 1-7pm Mon-Sat Ⓜ Alma-Marceau

GAY & LESBIAN PARIS

The Marais – especially the areas near the intersection of rue des Archives and rue Ste-Croix de la Bretonnerie (4e), and eastward to rue Vieille du Temple – has been Paris' hub of gay social life since the early 1980s. There are also some decent bars west of blvd de Sébastopol in the 1er and 2e.

Banana Café (5, C1)
This ever-popular, subtly named bar, was *the* male cruise bar in the late '90s and still attracts a buffed-up crowd to pick-up or just be mesmerised by the (weekend) go-go dancers. One of the only gay all-nighters, the two floors offer a constant turnover of talent.
☎ 01 42 33 35 31 ✉ 13

rue de la Ferronnerie, 1er ☾ 4pm-7am Ⓜ Châtelet-Les Halles

Bliss Kfé (5, D2)
This former patisserie is the setting for the most popular newcomer to the lesbian scene in the Marais area. A sophisticated, though not entirely Sapphic vibe, accompanies your

cocktails and there's a club downstairs that pulsates on both Friday and Saturday nights.
☎ 01 55 34 98 81 ✉ 30 rue du Roi-de-Sicile, 4e ☾ 5pm-2am Ⓜ St-Paul

Full Metal (5, D1)
Full Metal is a full-on, mens-only cruising bar and is hot 'n' heavy most nights

through to closing. Usually there's a fetish dress code – leather, rubber, sports attire, uniforms, (you get the picture) so plan ahead.
☎ 01 42 72 30 05 ⌨ www.fullmetal .fr in French ✉ 40 rue des Blancs Manteaux, 4e ⏰ 5pm-4am Sun-Thu, 5pm-6am Fri & Sat Ⓜ Rambuteau

Le Boobsberg (3, H3) This a relaxed and cosy lesbian bar and restaurant with decent food and good DJs, attracting locals and those who want to get away from the usual Marais scene.
☎ 01 42 74 04 82 ✉ 26 rue de Montmorency, 3e ⏰ 5.30pm-2am Tue-Sat Ⓜ Rambuteau

Le Cox (5, D1) Often the next stop after Open Café (right) on a gay boys' bar-hop, this kitschy wonder draws a cruisy crowd throughout the night. If you're doing the same, make a beeline for it during happy hour between 6pm to 9pm.
☎ 01 42 72 08 00 ✉ 15 rue des Archives, 4e ⏰ 1pm-2am

Ⓜ Hôtel de Ville
Le Pulp (3, G2) It's still Paris' main girls-only club, but the mixed nights (Wednesday and Thursday) are fun. On other nights there's lots of cruising, mostly on the weekends. Watch out for guest DJs.
☎ 01 40 26 01 93 ✉ 25 blvd Poissonière, 2e € €9-10; ⏰ midnight-6am Thu-Sun Ⓜ Grands Boulevards

Le Queen (3, B2) While it's still the Queen of gay discos, Le Queen is exploring its mixed crowd side, and there's nothing wrong with that. There are theme parties, but you'll have to check their listings for the exclusively gay nights.
☎ 01 53 89 08 90 ✉ 102 av des Champs Élysées, 8e € €10-20 depending on night (includes free drink) ⏰ midnight-dawn Ⓜ George V

Le Quetzal (5, D2) While it's lost some lustre, this dimly lit, modern bar still attracts a 30-something gay male crowd. It's free of

attitude, but still very cruisy, with a good happy hour between 5pm and 9pm.
☎ 01 48 87 99 07 ✉ 10 rue de la Verrerie, 4e ⏰ 5pm-5am Ⓜ Hôtel de Ville

Les Scandaleuses (5, D2) The place to go after Bliss Kfé (p93), Les Scandaleuses is a Marais lesbian mainstay, with an arty crowd and good cocktails. There's room to talk or dance when the weekend guest DJs are doing their thing. Accompanied men are welcome and happy hour is 6pm to 8pm.
☎ 01 48 87 39 26 ✉ 8 rue des Écouffes, 4e ⏰ 6pm-2am Ⓜ Hôtel de Ville

Open Café (5, D1) Great for a first drink on a night out or one enroute home (one will become a few), this is a great meeting place. Social rather than sexy, when it's fine weather the pavement is packed, mainly during happy hour (6pm to 9pm).
☎ 01 42 72 26 18 ✉ 17 rue des Archives, 4e ⏰ 10am-2am Ⓜ Hôtel de Ville

www.opencafe.tr

Cool, calm and collected – Open Café

SPORTS

For information on upcoming sporting events, consult the sports daily *L'Équipe* (www.lequipe.fr in French), or the *Le Figaro* entertainment supplement *Figaroscope* (www.figaroscope.fr), which is published each Wednesday.

Since 1974 the very last stage of the Tour de France, the world's most prestigious cycling event, has concluded on the av des Champs Élysées. The final day alternates from year to year but is commonly the afternoon of the third or fourth Sunday in July. The frenetic pace of track cycling speeds its way to the Palais Omnisports de Paris-Bercy (see p85) in winter with both the Grand Prix des Nations (October) and the Paris Six-Day (January).

Le foot (soccer) is very popular in France and Paris has its fair share of international events. The 80,000-seat Stade de France in St-Denis hosted the World Cup finals in 1998 (which France won) and is the major venue for soccer and rugby alike. Paris–St-Germain football team plays its home games at the Parc des Princes. The football played with the oval-shaped ball in France, rugby, is a popular sport and the local club is Le Racing Club de France, whose home ground is Stade Yves du Manoir in Colombe.

If you haven't splashed out sufficiently on restaurants and shopping, there are six racecourses located around Paris for your betting pleasure. The **Hippodrome d'Auteuil** (2, B4) is the most easily accessible, and features steeplechases from February to early July, as well as early September to early December. The minimum bet that you can place is a mere €2.

Show jumping is very popular in Paris and the Jumping International de Paris, held in March at the Palais Omnisports de Paris-Bercy, attracts legions of fans.

In late May/early June the world of tennis focusses on the clay surface of Stade Roland Garros in the Bois de Boulogne for the second of the four Grand Slam tournaments.

Sporting Venues
Paris is not a great sporting city, but it does have a few decent venues for major and international events.
- **Palais Omnisports de Paris-Bercy** (2, G5; ☎ 01 44 68 44 68; www.bercy.fr; blvd de Bercy, 12e; Ⓜ Bercy)
- **Parc des Princes** (2, B5; ☎ 01 42 30 03 60; www.psg.fr; 24 rue du Commandant-Guilbaud, 16e; Ⓜ Porte d'Auteuil)
- **Stade de France** (1, E2; ☎ 01 55 93 00 00; www.stadefrance.fr; rue Francis de Pressensé, St-Denis; Ⓡ RER line B or D to Stade de France)
- **Stade Roland-Garros** (2, G2; ☎ 01 47 43 48 00; www.frenchopen.org; 2 av Gordon Bennett, 16e; Ⓜ Porte d'Auteuil)

Sleeping

Two things to remember about Paris accommodation to avoid disappointment; book early and rooms are small. Good accommodation gets snapped up weeks, sometimes months in advance, especially for the peak tourist period between May and October. And in January and March Paris' better hotels are wall-to-wall with bony-hipped fashion models here for the shows. Rates can be reduced form November to March.

In Paris you need to disassociate size from quality when it comes to hotel rooms. Unless you're in a suite, you'll often be tripping over bags and standing bolt upright in a 'phone-box' sized shower. There are four basic types of accommodation: deluxe hotels, which are four-star 'L' (for *luxe*) in Paris. Paris has some gems in this range considered legendary for their décor and service, as well as a couple of chic newcomers. Top-end hotels mainly offer contemporary style with an excellent range of facilities such as WiFi (wireless Internet) and gyms. The midrange hotels are often situated in interesting neighbourhoods, but vary in the facilities on offer. Budget hotels in Paris offer no surprises apart from just how thin the 'walls' can be and still be called walls. Take earplugs.

Breakfast has not been included in the listed accommodation prices. Breakfast will cost you anywhere from €8 for coffee and pastries to between €25 and €30 for a hot breakfast, usually only offered in a deluxe hotel. Except for breakfast rooms offering wonderful ambience, you're better off hitting one of Paris' atmospheric cafés.

If you arrive in Paris without a room (what were you thinking!), the Paris tourism offices (p121) offer an accommodation service to locate you a room for the night.

Room Rates
The price ranges in this chapter indicate the cost per night of a standard double room. Seasonal variations can apply. Breakfast is excluded.

Deluxe	from €280
Top End	€160–280
Midrange	€90–160
Budget	under €90

Knock at your own peril at Artus Hôtel p98

JONATHAN SMITH

The booking fee depends on the level of accommodation – it's €8 for a four-star *luxe* hotel costing from €260 to €730.

Oh, and did we mention the two definite things to remember about Paris accommodation?

DELUXE

Four Seasons Hôtel George V (3, B2) You can be assured of royal treatment when visiting this opulent hotel – it's owned by a Saudi royal. The rooms are among the biggest in Paris, and there's an extravagant spa and excellent gym facilities to work off the food from Michelin three-star Le Cinq. The service is unsurpassed and children are most welcome.
☎ 01 49 52 70 00
🖳 www.fourseasons.com ✉ 31 av George V, 8e Ⓜ Victor Hugo 🔀 🖳 ✖ 🔁 🛉

Hôtel Costes (3, E2) The dark, opulent rooms of this boutique hotel are almost vampiric – perhaps fitting considering the hours kept by the stars that frequent it. Amenities are excellent; the restaurant shines, the pool is gorgeous, the bar legendary. If you actually bother to leave the hotel, it's perfectly positioned for the most chic of Paris' shopping.
☎ 01 42 44 50 00
🖳 www.hotelcostes.com ✉ 239 rue St-Honoré, 1er Ⓜ Concorde 🔀 🖳 🔁

Hôtel Meurice (3, E3) Having been completely renovated, this former palace is as fresh as the orchids in its gorgeous *jardin d'hiver* (winter garden). The hotel has entertained countless royals – none as demanding as Salvador Dalí whose order of a herd of sheep was fulfilled by the accommodating staff. Today it offers a lavish spa and creative cuisine at two-star Le Meurice. There's no pool, but you could try a Dalíesque request of one for your room – and probably get it.
☎ 01 44 58 10 10
🖳 www.meuricehotel.com ✉ 228 rue de Rivoli, 1e Ⓜ Tuileries 🔀 🖳 ✖

Hôtel Murano (3, J3) The newest addition to Paris' deluxe hotel scene, the fantastic Murano bills itself as an urban resort. White and bright, this sleek hotel has 43 rooms and nine amazing suites – some with their own lap pool. It's an audacious move in a city where some five-stars don't even have a pool in the hotel (let alone the room), so book now before the jet-set from Hôtel Costes (left) start spoiling it.
☎ 01 42 71 20 00
🖳 www.muranoresort.com ✉ 13 blvd du Temple, 3e Ⓜ Filles du Calvaire 🔀 🖳 🔁 ✖ 🔁 good

Hôtel Ritz (3, E2) César Ritz opened his 'perfect hotel' in 1898 and as a testament to his taste some discerning guests (such as Coco Chanel) now have suites named after them. All the mod-cons you would expect are here – hidden amid the sumptuousness of the rooms. Service is exemplary and taking a dip in the phenomenal pool and sipping champagne at Bar Vendôme is a must.
☎ 01 43 16 30 70
🖳 www.ritzparis.com ✉ 15 place Vendôme, 1er Ⓜ Opéra 🔀 🖳 🔁

Intercontinental Le Grand Hôtel (3, E2) Following its multimillion dollar, 18-month renovation, this 1862 Parisian landmark would earn approval from its original owner, Napoleon III. With 477 rooms, it's Paris' largest luxury

Feel like royalty in this former palace – Hôtel Meurice

JEAN-BERNARD CARILLET

hotel and while its been refurbished with welcome restraint, the fabulously ornate Opéra Salon and Grand Ballroom are still as breathtaking as ever.
☎ 01 40 07 32 32
🖳 www.ichotels group.com ✉ 2 rue Scribe, 9e Ⓜ Opéra
🔀 🖳 ✖ ☎

L'Hôtel (5, A2) Tucked away in a quiet quayside street, L'Hôtel is the stuff of romantic Paris legends. Rock and film star regulars compete to book Number 16 where Oscar Wilde took his last catnap. Service is consummate and the overwhelming baroque/ Empire décor almost takes your mind off the snugness of the rooms.
☎ 01 44 41 99 00
🖳 www.l-hotel.com
✉ 13 rue des Beaux Arts, 6e Ⓜ St-Germain des Prés 🔀 🖳 ☎

Rub shoulders with the literati – Oscar Wilde room, L'Hôtel

Park Hyatt Paris Vendôme (3, E2) Combining five office buildings leading off place Vendôme, this is a hip, minimalist Hyatt, which is the perfect antidote to the grand hotels. With quality fittings, Bang & Olufsen entertainment and high-speed Internet, it attracts a younger crowd than the other *luxe* hotels. Le Park restaurant provides fine contemporary cuisine.
☎ 01 58 71 12 34
🖳 www.paris.vendome .hyatt.com ✉ 5 rue de la Paix, 2e Ⓜ Opéra
🔀 🖳 ✖

TOP END

Arioso Hotel (3, D1) This late 18th-century building, a short hop from the Champs Élysées, is now an elegant 28-room hotel. The rooms (some with balconies) are all furnished in a tasteful, traditional style. All rooms have WiFi Internet, most are nonsmoking and some are disabled-friendly.
☎ 01 53 05 95 00
🖳 www.arioso-hotel .com ✉ 7 rue d'Argenson, 8e Ⓜ Miromesnil
🔀 🖳 ✖ ♿ good

ArtusHotel (2, A3) This intimate boutique hotel, with its graffiti-covered staircase

and modern artwork is only a stone's throw from place St-Germain des Prés. The small rooms (book a suite if possible) are comfortable and the hotel has a warm feel amplified by the helpful staff.
☎ 01 43 29 07 20
🖳 www.artushotel.com
✉ 34 rue de Buci, 6e
Ⓜ St-Germain des Prés
🔀 🖳

Hôtel Brighton (3, E3) The three-star Brighton, has 65 lovely rooms (many refurbished) and the rooms overlooking the Jardin des Tuileries are very popular;

those on the 4th and 5th floors afford views over the trees to the Seine. Service is friendly and relaxed.
☎ 01 47 03 61 61
🖳 www.esprit-de-france .com ✉ 218 rue de Rivoli, 1er Ⓜ Tuileries
🔀

Hôtel de Lutèce (5, D3) If the romantic notion of a stay on one of Paris' Îles (Islands) arouses your curiosity, this exquisite little hotel has just the right atmosphere on charming Île St-Louis (p15). The comfortable rooms are tastefully decorated, the staff friendly and the location is certainly delightful.

☎ 01 43 26 23 52; fax 01 43 29 60 25 ✉ 65 rue St-Louis en l'Île, 4e Ⓜ Pont Marie

Hôtel du Bourg Tibourg
(5, D2) Eclectic, funky and romantic, this intimate hotel was revamped by Jacques Garcia, of Hôtel Costes (p97) notoriety. Minimalists beware – barely a square centimetre of the small rooms has been left untouched by Garcia. It does have oodles of Oriental/neo-Gothic charm and it's in a great neighbourhood.
☎ 01 42 78 47 39
🖳 www.hoteldubourg tibourg.com ✉ 19 du Bourg Tibourg, 4e Ⓜ Hôtel de Ville, St-Paul 🗙 🖳

Hôtel Le A (3, C2) A stylish, minimalist hotel that doesn't have the 'attitude' that generally goes with it. White, black and grey all

over, the colour scheme accentuates the contemporary art and fresh flowers placed around the hotel. The airy spaces and fireplace are as welcome as the nonsmoking floor, but the rooms are petite (remember, this is Paris) and there's no gym.
☎ 01 42 56 99 99
🖳 hotel-le-a.com
✉ 4 rue d'Artois, 8e
Ⓜ Franklin D Roosevelt 🗙 🖳 🍴

Serviced Apartments
Serviced apartments are a great idea if you're lucky enough to be staying more than a week or two.
- **France Location** (☎ 01 44 89 66 70 🖳 www .franceloc.com) This chain of serviced apartments has properties around France, including Paris. A two-person studio is €497-574 per week, 4-person apartment €784-994 per week.
- **Paris Apartments Services** (☎ 01 40 28 01 28 🖳 www.paris-apts.com) Well-positioned three-star studio apartments from €92 per night and one-bedroom apartments from €134, mini mum of five nights stay.

Hôtel Le Clos Médicis
(5, B4) With a great combination of contemporary style and fabulous location, this is an excellent choice close to the Jardin de Luxembourg. The warm and welcoming lobby and sunken fireplace set the tone and even the 'classic' (standard) rooms are a comfortable size.
☎ 01 43 29 10 80
🖳 www.closmedicis .com ✉ 56 rue Monsieur-le-Prince, 6e 🚊 Luxembourg 🗙 🖳

Hôtel Victoires Opéra (3, G3) Right in the middle of a wonderful pedestrianised market street, this is an elegant, understated four-star hotel with a broad range of rooms. The hotel has been completely refurbished, the superior rooms are great and the deluxe ones overlook the street – yes, they are soundproofed.
☎ 01 42 36 41 08
🖳 www.hotelvictoires opera.com ✉ 56 rue de Montorgueil, 2e Ⓜ Sentier 🗙 🖳 ♿ good

Hôtel Le Clos Medicis – any link with Leonardo's patrons?

JEAN-BERNARD CARILLET

MIDRANGE

Hôtel Axial Beaubourg

(5, D1) The refit of this 16th-century building has struck a nice balance of modern fittings and original exposed beams and bare brick. It doesn't hide the snugness of the rooms, although its position in the heart of the Marais hints that you'll be spending more time out than in.
☎ 01 42 72 72 22
🖥 www.axialbeau
bourg.com ✉ 11 rue du Temple, 4e Ⓜ Hôtel de Ville 🌐 🖥

Hôtel Beaumarchais

(3, J3) This 31-room boutique hotel is well positioned for rue Oberkampf bars and boutiques. The rooms are starting to get a little frayed around the edges. Some rooms look on to a small leafy courtyard.
☎ 01 53 36 86 86
🖥 www.hotelbeau
marchais.com ✉ 3 rue Oberkampf, 11e Ⓜ Filles du Calvaire 🌐

Hôtel Caron de Beaumarchais

(5, D2) Beaumarchais, who wrote *Le Mariage de Figaro* (at No 47), is the theme character of this 18th century, 19-room charmer. While located in a wonderful street in the Marais, claustrophobics should take the streetside balconied rooms. WiFi Internet and flatscreen TVs in each room sweeten the deal.
☎ 01 42 72 34 12
🖥 www.carondebeau
marchais.com ✉ 12 rue Vieille-du-Temple, 4e Ⓜ St-Paul or Hôtel de Ville 🌐 🖥

Hôtel des Grandes Écoles

(3, G5) This 51-room hotel is tucked in a courtyard off a medieval street, just north of place de la Contrescarpe. The rooms have barely a surface without a pattern on them, but they suit the handsome building. Breakfast is in a pretty garden.
☎ 01 43 26 79 23
🖥 www.hotel-grandes
-ecoles.com ✉ 75 rue du Cardinal Lemoine, 5e Ⓜ Cardinal Lemoine

Hôtel La Manufacture

(2, F5) The graceful, minimalist La Manufacture is located on the fringe of the Latin Quarter in an interesting neighbourhood. The individually decorated rooms adhere to clean lines and the top-floor rooms are undoubtedly the most spacious.
☎ 01 45 35 45 25
🖥 www.hotel-la-manu
facture.com ✉ 8 rue Philippe de Champagne (av des Gobelins), 13e Ⓜ place d'Italie 🌐 🖥 🍽 ♿ limited

Hôtel Lenox Montparnasse

(3, E6) Taking its name from a Scottish aristocrat, this warm, welcoming hotel has some delightful Art Deco touches, including the popular bar. While the standard rooms are very snug, the 'Club'

Snuggle into 18th-century charm at Hôtel Caron de Beaumarchais

JEAN-BERNARD CARILLET

rooms are excellent and the suites are impressive.

☎ 01 43 35 34 50
🖳 www.hotellenox.com
✉ 15 rue Delambre, 14e
Ⓜ Vavin

Hôtel St-Germain des Prés (5, A2)

Located up from the cafés and clamour of place St-Germain des Prés, this well-appointed cosy hotel has individually decorated (if a little heavy-handed) rooms. The 'castle' suite is very romantic, there's free WiFi Internet, but usually people stay here for the great position.

☎ 01 40 46 83 63
🖳 www.hotel-paris-saint-germain.com
✉ 36 rue Bonaparte, 6e
Ⓜ St-Germain des Prés

Hôtel Verneuil (5, A2)

Chic and cosy, this small hotel has 26 rooms of individually decorated charm in a quiet street just off St-Germain des Prés. Well

Work, Pleasure or Leisure

Here's our list of the best hotels to suit your needs:

- **Business Trip** Park Hyatt Paris Vendôme (p98)
- **Location, Location, Location** Hôtel Axial Beaubourg (opposite)
- **Romantic Sojourn** Hôtel Ritz (p97)
- **Too Cool for School** Hôtel Costes (p97)

JEAN-BERNARD CARILLET

Make a splash at Hôtel Costes

suited to the surrounds, as galleries and antique shops abound In the area, there are original engravings and art on the walls. Just over

half the rooms in this 17th-century abode has air con.

☎ 01 42 60 83 14
🖳 www.hotelverneuil.com ✉ 8 rue de Verneuil, 7e Ⓜ St-Germain des Prés

Le Général Hôtel (3, J2)

This recently opened hotel close to the place de la Republique has excellent facilities for a three-star rating – such as a gym and sauna, WiFi Internet, business centre and bar. The hotel's décor, all white with touches of pink and fuchsia, is fresh and fun and the rooms are well soundproofed.

☎ 01 47 00 41 57
🖳 www.legeneralhotel.com ✉ 5/7 rue Rampon, 11e Ⓜ République

JEAN-BERNARD CARILLET

Unlock yourself at Hôtel Axial Beaubourg

BUDGET

Hôtel Chopin (3, F1) This two-star hotel was built within one of Paris' most alluring 19th-century *passages* (shopping arcades) and has undeniable, though increasingly faded, *belle époque* charm. The staff are welcoming, the breakfast worthwhile and the comfortable top floors are your best bet.
☎ 01 47 70 58 10; fax 01 42 47 00 70 ✉ 46 passage Jouffroy (entry 10 blvd Montmartre), 9e Ⓜ Grands Boulevards

Hôtel de Nevers (3, J2) While the resident cats might have more character than the rooms, the staff are just as friendly and it's just a short stroll from the Marais and Oberkampf areas. Good mix of singles/doubles/triples and gay friendly.
☎ 01 47 00 56 18 🖳 www.hoteldenevers.com ✉ 53 rue de Malte, 11e Ⓜ République

Hôtel des Arts (3, G2) While the hotel may have lost its former funkiness, this quality two-star hotel in a quiet little alley off rue du Faubourg Montmartre is still an excellent choice for this area. Though it only has 25 rooms there's a good mix of singles/doubles/triples.
☎ 01 42 46 73 30 🖳 hdag@free.fr 7 ✉ Cité Bergère, 9e Ⓜ Grands Boulevards

Hôtel Esmeralda (5, C3) Tucked away in a quiet street with views of Notre Dame, this renovated 19-room inn is about as central to the Latin Quarter as you're ever going to get. Its charm is no secret, so book well ahead.
☎ 01 43 54 19 20; fax 01 40 51 00 68 ✉ 4 rue St-Julien le Pauvre, 5e Ⓜ St-Michel

Hôtel Jeanne d'Arc (5, E2) This small, welcoming hotel near place du Marché Ste-Catherine is a great *pied-à-terre* (residence) for your forays to the museums, bars and Marais restaurants, Village St-Paul and Bastille. Summer visitors should note the lack of air-con.
☎ 01 48 87 62 11 🖳 www.hoteljeanne darc.com ✉ 3 rue de Jarente, 4e Ⓜ St-Paul

Hôtel St-Jacques (3, G5) This endearing 35-room hotel has balconies overlooking the Panthéon and the hotel looks better than when Audrey Hepburn and Cary Grant filmed *Charade* scenes here. Room 25 is the most popular for its long balcony. Note that the rooms can be a little noisy.
☎ 01 44 07 45 45 🖳 www.hotel-saint jacques.com ✉ 35 rue des Écoles, 5e Ⓜ Maubert-Mutualité

Hôtel Chopin – drift off in nocturnal bliss

JEAN-BERNARD CARILLET

About Paris

HISTORY

The Gauls & the Romans

The Île de la Cité was settled during the 3rd century BC by a tribe of Celtic–Gaul river-traders known as the Parisii. Centuries of conflict between the Gauls and Rome ended in 52 BC, when Julius Caesar's legions took control of the territory and established the town known as Lutetia on the island and the left (south) bank of the Seine.

In AD 508 the Frankish king Clovis I united Gaul as a kingdom and made Paris (as it became known) his capital. Despite a succession of raids by church-torching Vikings during the 9th century, Paris flourished as the centre of the Francia Kingdoms' politics, commerce, religion and culture.

The Middle Ages

In the 12th century, the construction of medieval landmark Cathédrale de Notre Dame was underway, the Right Bank was prospering as the town's mercantile centre, the food markets at Les Halles opened in 1110, and the Louvre was built as a riverside fortress around 1200. The Left Bank developed as a place of scholarship and learning (hence 'Latin' Quarter) and the Sorbonne opened its doors in 1253.

The Renaissance

After enduring the plague and the 'Hundred Years' War' with England, Paris lay in ruins and its kings eagerly embraced Italian Renaissance culture in the early 16th century. Many of the city's signature buildings and monuments were built during the period, including the Pont Neuf, the Église St-Eustache and the Hôtel Carnavalet. Henri IV (ruled 1589–1610) rebuilt Paris in grand style, including the magnificent place Royale (now place des Vosges) and place Dauphine.

Pont Neuf helped bridge the gap from ruined Paris to the city's Renaissance

Louis XIV & the Ancien Régime

Louis XIV, known as le Roi Soleil (the Sun King), ascended the throne in 1643 at the tender age of five but it wasn't until he was 24 that he asserted his rule and embarked on several wars. His other legacy was the splendid architecture; the palace at Versailles, place Vendôme, place des Victoires and the layout of the *grands boulevards* were commissioned

A century later, the extravagant ways of Louis XVI and his capricious queen, Marie-Antoinette, resulted in an uprising and, on 14 July 1789 mobs stormed the prison, the ultimate symbol of the despotism of the *ancien régime*. The French Revolution had commenced.

Revolution & Napoleon

The Revolution's moderate populist ideals at its early stages quickly gave way to the Reign of Terror,

Napolean's wins on Colonne Vendôme

with over 17,000 people introduced to *madame la guillotine,* including Louis XVI, his queen, and eventually many of the Revolution's original 'patriots' such as Robespierre.

The unstable post-Revolution government was consolidated in 1799 under a young Corsican general, Napoleon Bonaparte, who crowned himself 'Emperor of the French' at Notre Dame in 1804, and proceeded to sweep most of Europe under his wing. The Arc de Triomphe and the Code Napoléon (still the basis of the French legal system) are among his legacies.

The Second Empire

Following Napoleon's defeat at Waterloo and exile in 1815, France faltered under inept rulers until another revolution in 1848, which was followed by Napoleon III (nephew of Bonaparte) declaring himself emperor in a coup d'état in 1851. The Second Empire began and Napoleon III charged Baron Haussmann with the task of transforming Paris into the Paris we recognise today, with wide boulevards, fine public buildings and sculptured parks.

Napoleon III was less successful in his military operations and in 1870 he was captured during the Franco-Prussian war. Parisians took to the streets, demanding a republic, and a power struggle ensued between monarchists and the republicans of the Paris Commune, who briefly took over Paris.

The Belle Époque to the Present

Despite its bloody beginnings, the Third Republic ushered in the glittering *belle époque* (beautiful age), with its famed Art Nouveau architecture and quantum leaps in the arts and sciences. The Eiffel Tower, impressionism and the Paris of nightclubs and artistic cafés are legacies of this time. By the 1920s and '30s, Paris had become a worldwide centre for the artistic and intellectual avant-garde.

This exuberance was snuffed out by the Nazi occupation of Paris. Thousands of Jews living in Paris were sent to Nazi concentration and extermination camps. In August 1944, Hitler ordered his retreating army to raze the city; thankfully, his general refused.

After the war, a revitalised liberalism reached its crescendo in the student-led 'Spring Uprising' of May 1968, when some nine million people joined in a paralysing general strike sparked by opposition to the De Gaulle government and the Vietnam War.

During the 1980s, President François Mitterrand initiated his *grands travaux,* ambitious building projects that many consider his greatest legacy (p31). His successor, Jacques Chirac cemented his own legacy with his determined opposition to the US invasion of Iraq, an overwhelmingly popular stand within France. However, refusing to cut short his Canadian vacation while morgues overflowed with nearly 15,000 victims of the August 2003 heatwave was less than his finest hour.

> **Did You Know?**
> - Paris is the world's No 1 tourist destination: more than 36 million people visit Paris each year – 60% from other countries.
> - There are over 1450 hotels in Paris – and yet the one you want doesn't have a vacancy when you need one.
> - There are over 138,000 staff working in tourism-related activities.
> - Paris is underway with plans for a metro ferry service on the Seine.

Bibliothèque Nationale de France François Mitterand is book-shaped to entice the bookworms

ENVIRONMENT

For a densely populated urban hub, Paris is a surprisingly clean and healthy city. Thanks are due mainly to Baron Haussmann, who radically reshaped the city in the second half of the 19th century, widening streets, building parks, and modernising the sewer and storm-water systems.

Despite the city's excellent public transport system, Haussmann's wide boulevards are usually choked with traffic and air pollution is the city's major environmental hazard. Steps have been taken to reduce this – municipal buses run on electricity or natural gas and a network of extensive *vélo* (bicycle) lanes has been introduced.

Don't expect to escape pollution indoors, be prepared to inhale second-hand cigarette and cigar smoke pretty much everywhere (see p75). The new '100% *sans tabac*' campaign, which involves an inspection of the premises and the display of a blue label outside an establishment has yet to catch on.

Square du Vert Galant is the Seine's jewel

GOVERNMENT & POLITICS

Paris is the absolute centre of France's political scene and the politics of Paris affects the whole of France, as the saying goes, '*Quand Paris éternue, la France s'enrhume*' (when Paris sneezes, France catches cold). Paris is home to the French president (Jacques Chirac), the prime minister (Jean-Pierre Raffarin) and his government, the National Assembly, the Senate, the mayor of Paris (Bertrand Delanoë), the mayor's 18 *adjoints* (deputy

Secularism or Racism?

In arguably the most controversial and divisive issue the city and the nation have faced in decades, legislators voted 494 to 36 in February 2004 to ban Muslim headscarves and other religious apparel (including Jewish skullcaps and large Christian crosses) in public schools, despite protests that the measure infringes on religious freedom. While the move was said to promote secularism, it's clear that the largest affected group were young Muslim women, prompting calls of racism from many of France's six million Muslims.

mayors), the 163 members of the Conseil de Paris (Council of Paris), the mayors of each of the 20 *arrondissements* (plus their councils) and local European Parliament members.

Political debate is dominated by the right/left *(droite/gauche)*, conservative/socialist divide, and political players serve long apprenticeships. Chirac, for instance, was mayor of Paris and prime minister before being elected president. While Chirac's uneven popularity was given a boost by his stance on Iraq, his ability to secure a third term as president in 2007 is largely dependent on whether his popular former protégé, and president of the Union for a Popular Movement (UMP), Nicolas Sarkozy, decides to challenge. After forcing Sarkozy to leave his post as finance

More agitation on place de la Bastille

minister, Chirac is betting that Sarkozy's less public position with the UMP will keep his ambition at bay – at least in the short term.

ECONOMY

Paris is one of Europe's financial capitals and European headquarters to many multinational companies. It is also the heart of France's own commercial, industrial and financial sectors: about 20% of all economic activity in France takes place in the Paris region. A highly centralised

Commerce thrusts onwards and upwards at La Défense

bureaucracy means the capital also accounts for around 40% of the nation's white-collar jobs. More than 50% of GDP is spent by the government, which is by far the greatest employer of workers in Paris. The economy has fared reasonably well in recent years with unemployment falling from double-digits to around 9%.

SOCIETY & CULTURE

The population of Paris is about 2.1 million, while the Île de France (the greater metropolitan area of Paris) has about 11 million inhabitants – about 19% of France's total population of 58 million people. Paris today is a very cosmopolitan city, with many residents hailing from other nations of the EU.

In the second half of the 20th century France received waves of immigration, often from former French colonies in North Africa and French-speaking sub-Saharan Africa. This has prompted some paranoia that was milked by far-right politician Jean-Marie Le Pen with his Front National party getting six million votes in the presidential election of 2002. And while France has prided itself on its *égalité* (equality), job discrimination and other subtle forms of racism exist.

The French are generally more relaxed about relations between men and women – and about sex. Paris has thriving gay and lesbian communities, and same-sex couples are a common sight on its streets. Prostitution, although illegal, is widely tolerated.

> ### Some Useful Dos & Don'ts Include:
> - Always say *'Bonjour'* when entering a shop, and *'Merci, monsieur/madame/mademoiselle… au revoir'* when you leave.
> - If you want help or to interrupt someone, start with *'Excusez-moi, monsieur/madame/mademoiselle'*.
> - Friends exchange *bises* (kisses) as a greeting (including men if they are close friends). The ritual is one glancing peck on each cheek. People who don't kiss each other will often shake hands.

Etiquette/Dos & Don'ts

Although the stereotype of the haughty, arrogant and unwelcoming Parisian may have been accurate 20 years ago it's certainly not true today. Parisians tend to be shy with strangers, but will readily help if approached in a friendly manner – especially if you attempt to address them in French (see above).

Pull up a chair and relax with the locals

JONATHAN SMITH

ARTS

A century ago Paris held centre stage in the art world, attracting many of the painters, writers and musicians who forged the modern period. Paris has retained this reputation thanks in part to the city's peerless architectural beauty – evident in the ground-breaking Gothic Cathédrale de Notre Dame, ostentatiously baroque Palais du Luxembourg, seriously classical Panthéon and Arc de Triomphe, plus the Art Nouveau detailing on everything from metro entrances (p33) to bistros.

Cinema

The Lumière brothers perfected the Cinématographe system to produce 'moving pictures' in 1895. In the 1920s and '30s directors, such as René Clair, Marcel Carné as well as Jean Renoir, produced films that have become classics. In the late 1950s the *nouvelle vague* (new wave) of directors including Jean-Luc Godard and François Truffaut approached cinematography, editing and drama with a freshness that has influenced directors ever since. Godard's actors, Anna Karina (*Alphaville*) and Jean-Paul Belmondo (*À Bout de Souffle*) wrote the book on Parisian cool.

While Jean-Pierre Jeunet's 2001 *Le Fabuleux Destin d'Amélie Poulain* (Amélie from Montmartre) was a huge success, the expected French cinema revival is yet to happen.

Literature & Music

The country's literary legacy is equally statuesque, with prominent and influential writers such as Molière, Jean-Baptiste Racine, Voltaire, Jean-Jacques Rousseau, Victor Hugo, Honoré de Balzac, Émile Zola, Marcel Proust, Simone de Beauvoir and Albert Camus.

1756 · MOZART · 1791

JONATHAN SMITH

Theatrical highs and lows are etched into the Palais du Luxembourg

The 19th century saw the promotion of musical luminaries such as Hector Berlioz, César Franck, Georges Bizet, Claude Debussy, as well as Maurice Ravel. In the 20th century, jazz in Paris produced violinist Stéphane Grappelli and legendary Romany guitarist Django Reinhardt, while popular singers included the 'little sparrow' Édith Piaf, Jacques Brel and Serge Gainsbourg.

Today's scene sees artists such as Paris Combo reinventing traditional *chanson* (see p90), Gotan Project updating tango, Bertrand Burgalat reworking '60s pop and Mano Chao mixing rock/latin/reggae sung in French, Spanish and Arabic. French hip-hop has a superstar in rapper MC Solaar while Air and Cassius are still Paris' best electronic music exporters, but Paris' DJs appear to be stuck in a house and disco cul-de-sac.

Painting

According to author and philosopher Voltaire, French painting began in the 1600s with Nicolas Poussin and Claude Lorrain, painters of eerily light-drenched classical scenes. The neoclassical and Romantic movements rejected pastel hues, with Jacques Louis David and Théodore Géricault painting huge historical scenes.

Pastoral themes returned with the Barbizon School of Jean-Baptiste Camille Corot and Jean-François Millet, whose landscapes were painted in the outdoors, a novel concept for its time. Still outdoors and inspired by the fleeting effects of light were the impressionists, the movements' name given to them by their leading practitioner, Claude Monet in 1874. Some of the other luminaries of the movement were Alfred Sisley, Camille Pissarro and Auguste Renoir.

The artistic push continued and more movements followed, such as Symbolism (Gustave Moreau), Fauvism (Henri Matisse and André Derain), Cubism (Pablo Picasso and Georges Braque), Dadaism (Marcel Duchamp) and its offshoot surrealism, led by Paris-based Spaniard Salvador Dalí. WWII, however, effectively burst the creative bubble of Paris' art scene and it's never returned to the level of innovative energy that it once had.

Inspiration in Paris

Many English-speaking writers have found their muse in Paris, beginning with Charles Dickens whose *A Tale of Two Cities* (1859) is a fascinating account of the French Revolution. Hemingway's *A Moveable Feast* (1961) portrays 1920s bohemian life in Paris, and his sometime friend Gertrude Stein's *The Autobiography of Alice B Toklas* (1933) is a fascinating account of the author's years in Paris and her friendships with Matisse, Picasso, Braque and Hemingway. George Orwell's *Down and Out in Paris and London* (1940) includes an entertaining account of his time as a penniless dishwasher in Paris. *Tropic of Cancer* and *Quiet Days in Clichy* by Henry Miller are steamy autobiographical novels set in the French capital, published in France in the 1930s but banned in many other countries.

Directory

Art springs from the pavement on Monmartre's place du Tertre

JEAN-BERNARD CARILLET

ARRIVAL & DEPARTURE

Air

Two major international airports serve Paris, both are well connected to the city by train, bus and taxi. A third airport, Paris Beauvais, handles flights by some charter companies and Ryanair.

AÉROPORT D'ORLY

This smaller airport (1, E2) is 18km south of the city centre. It has two terminals – Ouest (West; mainly domestic flights) and Sud (South; some international flights), linked by the free Orlyval shuttle train.

Information

General inquiries (☎ 01 49 75 15 15)
Flight information (🖥 www.adp.fr)

Airport Access

Train The **Orlyval shuttle train** (☎ 08 92 68 77 14; 🕑 6am-11pm) links Orly with RER line B at Antony (8 minutes), every 7 minutes. From Antony it's a 35-minute trip to central Paris (€8.80, one way).

Bus Linking the airport with place Denfert Rochereau (2, E5), the **Orlybus** (☎ 08 92 68 77 14; € one way €5.70; 🕑 6am-11pm) runs every 15 minutes.

Shuttle The **Air France shuttle** (☎ 08 92 35 08 20; one way/return €7.50/12.75; 🕑 6am-11pm) runs services from the airport to Gare Montparnasse and Aérogare des Invalides (30 minutes) every 15 minutes. **Paris Airports Service** (☎ 01 49 62 78 78; single/2-plus passengers €22/13.50) provides door-to-door service. Pre-booking is required.

Taxi The tariff to the city is €40 (depending on time of day) and there is a charge of €1 per luggage item. It takes up to 30 minutes.

AÉROPORT PARIS-BEAUVAIS

This **airport** (BVA; ☎ 03 44 11 46 86; www.aeroportbeauvais.com) is 80km north of Paris.

Information

Flight information (🖥 www .aeroportbeauvais.com)
General inquiries (☎ 08 92 68 20 64)

Airport Access

Bus Express services leave the airport about 20 to 30 minutes after each flight arrival, from 5.45am to 7.15pm, and drop passengers on Place de la Porte Maillot (2, C2). Buses leave Paris for the airport three hours and 15 minutes before flight departure at **Parking Pershing** (2, C2; 1 blvd Pershing, 17e; Ⓜ Porte Maillot). Tickets (€10 one way) are available at **Ryanair** (☎ 03 44 11 41 41) at the airport or they can be purchase from a kiosk in the parking lot.

Taxi Between the city and Beauvais, taxis cost €110 (day) and €150 (night and all day Sunday).

AÉROPORT ROISSY CHARLES DE GAULLE

Paris' main international airport (1, EJ), 30km northeast of the city centre is generally referred to as Charles de Gaulle (CDG). There are two main terminals, CDG1 and CDG2 and a free *navette* (shuttle bus) runs every 6 minutes between the two terminals.

Information

Flight information (🖥 www.adp.fr)
General inquiries (☎ 01 48 62 22 80 in English)

Airport Access

Train Leaving every 15 minutes, Roissyrail trains (RER line B) run from 5.30am to midnight (€7.75, one way) and take 40 minutes to the centre of Paris. If you're planning to use public transport widely, consider purchasing a Paris Visite Pass (p114). The RER station is accessed from CDG2.

Bus Services run by **Roissybus** (☎ 08 92 68 77 14; €8.20 one way; ☽ 5.45am-11pm) connect the airport with rue Scribe, place de l'Opéra (3, E2). Trips take at least 45 minutes.

Shuttle Door-to-door-service is provided by **Paris Airports Service** (☎ 01 55 98 10 80; single/2-plus passengers €24/14.50). Prebooking is required.

Taxi The tariff to the city is from €35 to €50, with the trip taking 30 to 50 minutes. There is a charge of €1 per luggage item.

Train
Paris has six major train stations, each with its own metro station: Gare d'Austerlitz (2, G5; 13c), Gare de l'Est (2, G5; 10e), Gare de Lyon (2, G2; 12e), Gare du Nord (10e), Gare Montparnasse (2, E5; 15e) and Gare St-Lazare (2, E2; 8c). Information for **SNCF** (Société Nationale des Chemins de Fer; ☎ 08 92 35 35 35; www.sncf.com) is available by phone or via the Internet .

The **Eurostar service** (☎ 08 36 35 35 39; UK ☎ 09 90 186 186; www.eurostar.com) runs between Paris Gare du Nord and London's Waterloo Station taking between 2½ hours and three hours.

Bus
Eurolines (5, C3; ☎ 01 43 54 11 99, 08 92 89 90 91; www.eurolines.com; 55 rue St-Jacques, 5e; Ⓜ Cluny La Sorbonne) has services operating throughout Europe. The **Gare Routière Internationale de Paris-Galliéni** (2, J3; ☎ 08 92 89 90 91; 28 av du Général de Gaulle; Ⓜ Gallieni), Paris' international

bus terminal, is in the inner suburb of Bagnolet.

Travel Documents
PASSPORT
Visitors must carry their passport or European Union (EU) national ID card at all times.

VISA
Visas are not required by citizens of Australia, Canada, the EU, New Zealand and USA (for visits up to three months). Everyone else (apart from nationals of some other European countries including Switzerland) requires a 'Schengen Visa' which is valid for most of Western Europe. Visas are available through French consulates.

Customs & Duty Free
You can no longer buy goods at duty-free prices if travelling only between the countries belonging to the EU.

The regular import allowances apply: tobacco (200 cigarettes, 50 cigars or 250g of loose tobacco), alcohol (1L of spirits or 2L of less than 22% alcohol by volume; 2L of wine), coffee (500g or 200g of extracts) as well as perfume (50g of perfume and 250mL of eau de toilette).

Left Luggage
Airports do not provide left-luggage facilities. However, all the major train stations have left-luggage offices. For a medium/large/extra large bag, they cost €3.40/5/7.50 for 48 hours. After that period, it costs €4.50 per day. It is worth noting that most left-luggage offices are closed from 11.15pm to 6.45am.

GETTING AROUND
Paris has a fast, efficient and safe public transit system operated by **RATP** (Régie Autonome des Transports Parisians; www.ratp.fr

in French). In this book, the nearest metro station is noted after the icon Ⓜ in each listing.

Travel Passes

Mobilis and Paris Visite passes are valid on the metro, RER, SNCF's suburban lines, buses, night buses, trams and covers the Montmartre funicular railway as well. The Mobilis card coupon allows unlimited travel for one day in two to eight zones (€5.20 to €18.30). It is available at all metro and RER stations, as well as SNCF stations in the Paris region.

Paris Visite passes offer discounted entry to selected attractions and discounts on transport fares. They cover different travel zones (divided into three, five or eight zones). The version that allows access from one to three zones costs €8.35/13.70/18.25/26.65 for one/two/three/five days. The passes are sold at larger metro and RER stations, SNCF offices in Paris, and at the airports.

Metro & RER

Paris' underground network is the fastest way of getting around the city. It has two separate but linked systems: the **metro** (Métropolitain shortened to *métro*) which has 14 lines and 372 stations; and the **RER** (Réseau Express Régional), a network of five suburban services (designated A to E) that pass through the city centre. Generally you use the RER to cover large distances quickly. There's a metro map inside the front cover of this book and free metro/RER maps are available at metro ticket windows.

The metro is open from 5.30am to 12.30am; trains run every five minutes or so. Each line is marked by a number, colour and direction (or final destination).

For information on the metro, RER and bus systems, call **RATP** (☎ 08 92 68 77 14 in French, ☎ 08 92 68 41 14 in English; www.ratp.fr in French ⏲ 6am-9pm). Tickets for travel within the Paris city limits on the metro and RER network cost €1.30 and €10 for a *carnet* (book) of 10. Children under four travel free; children under 11 half-fare.

Bus

Bus services run frequently from 5.45am to 8.30pm, but the number of routes is reduced at night and on Sundays. The Noctambus network operates after the metro has closed for the night. Buses, marked with a black owl in front of a yellow moon, depart every hour on the half-hour from 1am to 5.30am and they leave from just west of the Hôtel de Ville (3, G4). The service's 18 lines cover most of the city. Tickets cost €2.50 per journey and Mobilis or Paris Visite passes are valid.

Taxi

Taxis in Paris are plentiful and the optimum place to pick one up is at the ranks usually found adjacent to major intersections, although you can hail them. The *prise en charge* (flag fall) is €2. Within the city, it costs €0.62 per km for travel between 7am and 7pm Monday to Saturday (*Tarif A*; white light on meter), and €1.06 per km from 7pm to 7am, all day Sunday and public holidays (*Tarif B*; orange light on meter). Travel in the suburbs *(Tarif C)* costs €1.24 per km.

There is a €2.60 surcharge for taking a fourth passenger, but generally drivers refuse to accept more than three people for insurance purposes. Each luggage item that weighs over 5kg costs €1 and pick-ups from SNCF mainline stations cost another €0.70. It's a worthwhile idea to have your destination written down if you're unable speak French fluently.

A selection of radio-dispatched taxi companies, on call 24 hours, include:

Alpha Taxis (☎ 01 45 85 85 85)
Artaxi (☎ 01 42 41 50 50)
Taxis Bleus (☎ 01 49 36 10 10)

PRACTICALITIES
Business Hours
It's always a good idea to check the opening hours of any place you plan to visit in Paris before heading off. Many places are closed on Sunday and either Monday or Tuesday; many also close for lunch (12.30pm to 2.30pm). Many restaurants close before 11pm. Many museums have *nocturnes* (late opening hours) at least one night per week. Some shops open on Sunday mornings from July to August and to 10pm once a week, generally Thursday. Banks open from 9am to 4pm (some close for lunch).

Climate & When to Go
Paris is worth visiting at any time of the year, but April to May, and September are the preferred months weather-wise. However, the weather is always unpredictable. Most residents flee the city and many businesses close in August.

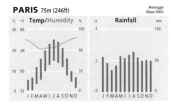

Disabled Travellers
France is not particularly well equipped for the *handicapés* (disabled people): kerb ramps are rare, older public facilities and midrange and budget hotels often lack lifts, and the Paris metro, most of it built decades ago, is particularly troublesome. But physically challenged people who want to visit Paris can overcome these problems. Most hotels with two or more stars are equipped with lifts but most are only just big enough to accommodate a *fauteuil roulent* (wheelchair). We've noted hotels with lifts and facilities for disabled people using the ♿ icon.

INFORMATION & ORGANISATIONS
The tourist office's website (www.parisinfo.com) lists organisations, plus some sights, accommodation and restaurants with the 'Tourisme & Handicap' sign, showing special facilities for the disabled. Contact **SNCF Accessibilité Service** (☎ 08 00 00 15 47 53) for advice on planning your journey.

For details on accessing the Paris region's public transport options, get a copy of the *Guide Practique à l'Usage des Personnes à Mobilité Réduite* from the **Syndicat des Transports d'Île de France** (☎ 01 47 53 28 00; www.stif-idf.fr).

Discounts
Concessions (usually 30 to 50%) abound for youth, students and seniors on everything from transport to museums. Bring whatever concession ID that you have from home and flash it every time you pull out your wallet.

Electricity
Voltage is 220V AC, 50Hz. Plugs in Paris generally have two round pins. Appliances rated US 110V need a transformer to work safely in Paris, and these (as well as adapters) can be bought at FNAC in Forum des Halles (5, C1) and BHV near Hôtel de Ville (3, G4).

Embassies
Australia (3, A4; ☎ 01 40 59 33 00; 4 rue Jean Rey, 15e; Ⓜ Bir Hakeim)

Canada (3, C2; ☎ 01 44 43 29 00; 35 ave Montaigne, 8e; Ⓜ Alma Marceau)
New Zealand (3, A2; ☎ 01 45 01 43 43; 7ter rue Léonard de Vinci, 16e; Ⓜ Victor Hugo)
South Africa (3, C3; ☎ 01 53 59 23 23; 59 Quai d'Orsay, 7e; Ⓜ Invalides)
UK (3, D2; ☎ 01 44 51 31 00; 35 rue du Faubourg St-Honoré, 8e; Ⓜ Concorde)
USA (3, D2; 2 av Gabriel, 8e; ☎ 01 43 12 21 72; Ⓜ Concorde)

Emergencies

To avoid being targeted by pickpockets in busy places, don't appear like the obvious tourist. The metro is safe until it closes, but stations which are better to avoid late at night include Châtelet-les Halles, Château Rouge in Montmartre, Gare du Nord, Strasbourg St-Denis, Réaumur Sébastopol and Montparnasse Bienvenüe. *Bornes d'alarme* (alarm boxes) are placed in the centre of each metro/RER platform.

Ambulance (☎ 15)
Police (☎ 17)
Fire Brigade (☎ 18)
Rape Crisis Hotline
(☎ 08 00 05 95 95)
SOS Helpline (☎ 01 47 23 80 80)

Fitness
CYCLING & SKATING

Including tracks in the Bois de Boulogne (2, A4; 16e) and Bois de Vincennes (2, J5; 12e), Paris now has extensive bicycle lanes throughout the city, as well as a dedicated lane running parallel to two-thirds of the blvd Périphérique. On Sundays and holidays almost all year, large sections of road are reserved for pedestrians, cyclists and skaters under a scheme called *Paris Respire* (Paris Breathes). For information on guided bicycle tours in Paris, see p47.

Inline skating is also very popular in Paris, see p37 for more information.

GYMS & FITNESS CLUBS

The two chains listed are the best bet for gym junkies. Note that both were opening new outlets at the time of writing, so check their websites for the latest branches. For spas, see p29.

Club Med Gym – Palais Royal
(5, B1; ☎ 01 40 20 03 03 🖳 www
.clubmedgym.com in French; 147 bis rue St-Honoré, 1er; single/10-entry *carnet* €40/320; 🕑 7.30am-10pm Mon-Fri, 9am-7pm Sat, 9am-5pm Sun Ⓜ Palais Royal-Musée du Louvre) A well-equipped chain with a dozen outlets.
Espace Vit' Halles (5, D1; ☎ 01 42 77 21 71; 🖳 www.vithalles.fr; 48 rue Rambuteau, 3e; single/10-entry *carnet* €25/179; 🕑 8am-10.30pm Mon-Fri, 10am-7pm Sat, 10am-6pm Sun; Ⓜ Rambuteau) Well-attended exercise classes and several other branches in Paris.

RUNNING

The best spots for an uninterrupted run are the Jardin du Luxembourg (3, F5) and along the Promenade Plantée (2, H4).

SWIMMING

Paris has over 30 public swimming pools; check with the **Mairie de Paris** (☎ 08 20 00 75 75; www.paris .fr) for a nearby pool. Most are short-length pools and lanes are as crowded as the Parisian streets. During school semesters avoid Wednesday afternoon and Saturday.

Aquaboulevard (2, C5; ☎ 01 40 60 10 00; www.aquaboulevard.com; 4 rue Louis Armand, 15e; adult/child 3-12 €20/10; 🕑 9am-11pm Mon-Thu, 9am-midnight Fri, 8am-midnight Sat, 8am-11pm Sun; Ⓜ Balard) A great one for families, this centre has a swimming pool, a 'beach', an aquatic park, tennis, squash, golf practise, gym and restaurants.

Piscine Pontoise-Quartier Latin (5, D3; ☎ 01 55 42 77 88; 18 rue de Pontoise, 5e; single/10-entry carnet €3.40/28.20; ⌚ 7-8.30am Mon-Fri, 12.15-1.30pm & 4.30-11.45pm Mon & Tue, 12.15-11.45pm Wed, 12.15-1.30pm, 4.30-7.15pm & 9-11.45pm Thu, noon-1.30pm, 4.30-8pm & 9-11.45pm Fri, 10am-7pm Sat, 8am-7pm Sun; Ⓜ Maubert-Mutualité) This beautiful Art Deco–style pool in the heart of the Latin Quarter measures 33m by 15m.

Piscine Suzanne Berlioux (3, F3; ☎ 01 42 36 98 44; Lvl 3, Forum des Halles, 10 place de la Rotonde, 1er; €3.80/3, under 4 free, 10-entry carnet €35/28.95; ⌚ 11.30am-10pm Mon, Tue, Thu & Fri, 10am-10pm Wed, 9am-7pm Sat & Sun; Ⓜ Les Halles) This 50m by 20m pool is in the bowels of Paris' largest shopping centre, and yes, people can see in!

Gay & Lesbian Travellers

With legal consent starting at 16 and enlightened laws regarding gay couples' rights introduced in 1999, France is one of Europe's most liberal countries. Paris has an openly gay mayor in Bertrand Delanoë and the gay scene is vibrant. The last couple of years has seen the lesbian scene blossom. For information on where to go out, see p93.

Health
MEDICAL SERVICES

Travel insurance is advisable to cover any medical treatment you may require while in Paris. EU residents who have a health insurance card are covered for emergency medical treatment throughout countries belonging to the EU. The coverage provided by most private US health insurance policies continues if you travel abroad, at least for a limited period.

There are more than 50 *assistance publique* (public health service) hospitals in Paris. If you're needing urgent attention, here are some possibilities:

Hôpital Américain (2, C1; ☎ 01 46 41 25 25; 63 blvd Victor Hugo, 17e; Ⓜ Porte Maillot)

Hôtel Dieu (5,C2; ☎ 01 42 34 81 31; place du Parvis Notre Dame, 4e; Ⓜ Cité)

SOS Médecins (☎ 01 47 07 77 77; ⌚ 24hr)

Urgences Médicales (☎ 01 48 28 40 04; ⌚ 24hr)

DENTAL SERVICES

These dental surgeries provide extended hours:

La Pitié-Salpêtrière (3, J6; ☎ 01 42 16 00 00; rue Bruand, 13e; Ⓜ St-Marcel)

SOS Dentaire (2, F5; ☎ 01 47 07 33 68; 87 blvd de Port Royal, 13e; Ⓜ Port Royal)

PHARMACIES

Some chemists with longer opening hours:

Dérhy/Pharmacie des Champs (3, B2; ☎ 01 45 62 02 41; Gallerie de Champs, 84 av des Champs Élysées, 8e; ⌚ 24hr; Ⓜ George V)

Pharmacie des Halles (5, C1; ☎ 01 42 72 03 23; ✉ 10 blvd de Sébastopol, 4e; ⌚ 9am-midnight Mon-Sat, 9am-10pm Sun; Ⓜ Châtelet)

Pharmacie Européenne de la Place de Clichy (4, A3; ☎ 01 48 74 65 18; 6 place de Clichy, 17e; ⌚ 24hr; Ⓜ place de Clichy)

Holidays

Paris has the following *jours fériés* (public holidays):

Jan 1	New Year's Day (Jour de l'An)
late Mar/Apr	Easter Sunday (Pâques)
late Mar/Apr	Easter Monday (Lundi de Pâques)
May 1	May Day (Fête du Travail)
May 8	Victoire 1945 (Victory in Europe Day)
May	Ascension Thursday (L'Ascension)
May/June	Whit Sunday/ Whit Monday (Pentecôte/ Lundi de Pentecôte)
July 14	Bastille Day (Fête Nationale)
Aug 15	Assumption Day (L'Assomption)
Nov 1	All Saints' Day (La Toussaint)
Nov 11	Armistice Day (Le Onze Novembre)
Dec 25	Christmas Day (Noël)

Internet
INTERNET CAFÉS

Some metro and RER stations provide free Internet access, but there is invariably a huge queue. About 50-odd post offices in Paris have Internet centres called **Cyberposte** (www.laposte.net in French). Many hotels and some cafés have started to offer wireless Internet for those wielding a wireless-equipped laptop. Internet café prices start at €3 per hour and the best and most central Internet cafes are:

Access Academy (5, B2; ☎ 01 43 25 23 80; 60-61 rue St-André des Arts, 6e; ☾ 8-2am; Ⓜ Odéon)

XS Arena Luxembourg (3, F5; ☎ 01 43 44 55 55; 17 rue Soufflot, 5e; ☾ 24hr; Ⓜ Luxembourg)

USEFUL WEBSITES

For information and links to useful travel resources start at the **Lonely Planet's websites** (www .lonelyplanet.com in English, www .lonelyplanet.fr in French). You could also try the following:

Mairie de Paris (www.paris.fr) Statistics and city information direct from the Hôtel de Ville.

Paris Tourist Office (www.parisinfo .com) The official tourism website.

Lost Property

All lost objects found anywhere in Paris (except those discovered on trains or in train stations) are eventually brought to the city's **Bureau des Objets Trouvés** (Lost Property Office; 2, D5; ☎ 01 55 76 20 20; fax 01 40 02 40 45; 36 rue des Morillons, 15e; ☾ 8.30am-5pm Mon & Wed, to 8pm Tue & Thu, to 5.30pm Fri Sep-Jun, to 7pm Mon-Fri Jul & Aug; Ⓜ Convention) operated by the Préfecture de Police.

Items mislaid on the metro are looked after by **station agents** (☎ 01 44 68 20 20) for three days, before being forwarded to the Bureau des Objets Trouvés. Anything found on trains or stations is taken to the lost-property office of the relevant station. Phone inquiries (in French) to locate items are possible.

Money
CURRENCY

Since 18 February 2002 the sole legal tender in France has been the euro (€), which is divided into 100 cents. Coins come in denominations of €1 and €2, and 1, 2, 5, 10, 20 and 50 cents. Notes come in denominations of €5, €10, €20, €50, €100, €200 and €500.

TRAVELLERS CHEQUES

Generally the most flexible travellers cheques are issued by American Express (in US dollars or euros) and Visa, as they can be changed at many post offices.

Amex offices don't charge commission on their own travellers cheques (though they charge about 4% on other brands). For lost or stolen Amex travellers cheques in Paris, call ☎ 08 00 90 86 00 (toll free ☯ 24hr). You can be reimbursed at **Amex** (3, E2; ☎ 01 47 14 50 00; 11 rue Scribe, 9e; ☯ 9.30am-7.30pm Mon-Fri Jun-Sep, to 6.30pm Oct-May, 9am-5.30pm Sat; Ⓜ Auber).

Thomas Cook (☎ 08 00 90 83 30; ☯ 24hr) has a toll-free customer service bureau.

CREDIT CARDS

Visa is the most widely accepted credit card, followed by Master-Card. American Express and Diners Club cards are only accepted at the more exclusive establishments. Many restaurants still don't accept credit cards, so keep some euros on hand. For lost cards contact:

Amex (☎ 01 47 77 72 00, 01 47 77 70 00)

Diners Club (☎ 08 10 31 41 59)

MasterCard (☎ 08 00 90 23 90, 01 45 67 53 53)

Visa/Carte Bleue (☎ 08 92 70 57 05, 08 92 69 08 80)

ATMS

Most ATMs in Paris are linked to the Cirrus and/or Maestro networks, but many ATMs won't accept PIN codes with more than four digits – ask your bank how to handle this before you leave.

CHANGING MONEY

Major train stations and hotels have exchange facilities operating evenings, weekends and holidays.

Many post offices provide transactions for a reasonable rate, but commercial banks generally charge €3 to €4.50 per transaction.

Exchange bureaux are faster, easier, open longer hours and give better rates than most banks. Here are some of the better ones open from 10am to 6pm:

Le Change du Louvre (5, B1; ☎ 01 42 97 27 28; 151 rue St- Honoré, 1er; Ⓜ Palais Royal-Musée du Louvre)

Thomas Cook (3, B1; ☎ 01 47 20 25 14 125; av des Champs-Elysées, 8e; Ⓜ Charles de Gaulle-Étoile)

Photography & Video

Print and slide film are both widely available and easily processed. For digital photography and video needs, FNAC (p50) has an excellent range of memory cards and other accessories. France uses the PAL (Phase Alternative Line) video system.

Newspapers & Magazines

The city's main daily newspapers are the conservative *Le Figaro*, the sombre, centre left–leaning *Le Monde* and arty, left-leaning *Libération*. The most popular weekly magazines are *L'Express*, *Le Nouvel Observateur* and *Le Point*.

English-language newspapers widely available in Paris are the *Economist*, *Financial Times*, *International Herald Tribune*, *Newsweek*, *Guardian*, *The Times*, *Time* and *USA Today*.

Post

The **main post office** (La Poste; 3, F3; ☎ 01 40 28 20 00; 52 rue du Louvre, 1er; Ⓜ Les Halles) is open 24 hours for mail services.

Each *arrondissement* has a five-digit postcode, beginning with 750 and ending with the *arrondissement* number, so 75001 for the *premièr arrondissement* (1er), 75019 for the

19e. The 16e has two postcodes: 75016 and 75116.

POSTAL RATES

Stamps are sold at *bureaux de poste* (post offices) and at some *tabacs* (tobacconists). Domestic/international letters (weighing up to 50g) cost €0.75/1.80.

Radio

The Radio France network offers several quality services in French, the best are: France Inter (opinion and music, 87.8FM), France Info (news and views, 105.5FM), France Culture (talk, 93.5/93.9FM), Paris Jazz (jazz and blues, 98.1FM) and Radio FG (club news and gigs, 98.2 FM). A mix of BBC World Service and BBC for Europe is at 648AM.

Telephone

French telephone numbers generally have 10 digits, the first two being the area code. For calls within France dial all 10 digits.

PHONECARDS

Most public telephones require a phonecard (*télécarte*) which can be purchased at post offices, *tabacs*, supermarkets, SNCF ticket windows, Paris metro stations and places displaying a blue sticker *'télécarte en vente ici'*. Cards worth 50 calling units cost €7.50; those worth 120 units are €15.

MOBILE PHONES

France uses the GSM 900/1800 cellular phone system, compatible with phones sold in the UK, Australia and most of Asia, but not those from North America or Japan – unless you have purchased a tri-band phone.

USEFUL NUMBERS

Directory assistance (local) (☎ 12)
Directory assistance (international) (☎ 00 33 12)
International Operator (☎ 00 33)

Television

There are five free-to-air television channels; three of which are state-owned (France 2, FR3 and Arte/France 5) and two are commercial networks (TF1 and M6). France 2 has a wide mix of programming, from game shows to drama; popular TF1 only interrupts game shows and reality television for football; M6 attracts a youthful audience with imported shows and local news, FR3 is the most 'serious' of French channels offering in-depth news and quality programming. Arte/France 5 offers educational shows by day and quality news, discussions and films by night.

Time

France is one hour ahead of GMT/UTC. During daylight-saving periods (last Sunday in March to the last Sunday in October) it is two hours ahead.

Tipping

French law requires that restaurant, café and hotel bills include a mandatory *service compris* (service charge) of approximately 12% to 15%. A *pourboire* (tip) is neither necessary nor expected. However, most people leave a few euros in good restaurants, unless the service was bad. In cafés, people occasionally leave small change as a tip, but it is not necessary if you have only consumed a coffee or a drink.

Toilets

Public toilets are signposted as *toilettes* or WC. Paris' pavement coin-operated public toilets are cheap, clean and there are lots of them located around the city. Open 24 hours, you get 15 minutes of toilet time for just €0.40, and the entire unit is automatically cleaned and disinfected after each visit. An adult should accompany children under 10. If you are not a paying customer, café owners disapprove of you using their facilities.

Tourist Information

The main branch of the **Office de Tourisme et de Congrès de Paris** (Paris Convention & Visitors Bureau; 3, E2; ☎ 08 92 68 30 00; www.parisinfo.com; 25-27 rue des Pyramides, 1er; ☒ 9am-8pm Apr-Oct, 9am-8pm Mon-Sat & 11am-7pm Sun Nov-Mar, closed 1 May; Ⓜ Pyramides) is located approximately 500m northwest of the Louvre.

The bureau also maintains five centres (telephone numbers and website are the same as the main office) elsewhere in Paris. Note that the offices are often closed on public holidays

Eiffel Tower (3, A2; Pilier Nord, Parc du Champ de Mars, 7e; ☒ 11am-6.45pm 2 May-Sep; Ⓜ Champ de Mars-Tour Eiffel)

Gare de Lyon (3. J6; Hall d'Arrivée, 20 blvd Diderot, 12e; ☒ 8am-6pm Mon-Sat; Ⓜ Gare de Lyon)

Gare du Nord (2, F2; 18 rue de Dunkerque, 10 ☒ 12.30-8pm; Ⓜ Fare du Nord)

Montmartre (4, D2; 21 place du Tertre, 18e; ☒ 10am-7pm; Ⓜ Abbesses)

Opéra/Grands Magasins (3, E2; 11 rue Scribe, 9e ☒ 9am-6.30pm Mon-Sat; Ⓜ Auber or Opéra)

LANGUAGE

Parisians are well used to English-speaking visitors, but you'll find that you receive a much warmer response if you begin a question with whatever French you can muster, even if it's simply 'Excusez-moi, madame/monsieur, parlez-vous anglais?' ('Excuse me, madam/sir, do you speak English?').

For more useful words and phrases, see Lonely Planet's *Fast Talk French*.

BASICS

Yes.	*Oui.*
No.	*Non.*
Maybe.	*Peut-être.*
Please.	*S'il vous plaît.*
Thank you.	*Merci.*
You're welcome.	*Je vous en prie.*
Excuse me.	*Excusez-moi.*
Sorry/Forgive me.	*Pardon.*
Hello/	
Good morning.	*Bonjour.*
Good evening/	*Bonsoir/*
night/	*Bonne nuit/*
bye.	*Au revoir.*
How are you?	*Comment allez-vous?* (polite); *Comment vas-tu?/ Ça va?* (informal)
Fine, thanks.	*Bien, merci.*
My name is …	*Je m'appelle …*
I'm pleased to meet you.	*Enchanté/e.* (m/f)
I understand.	*Je comprends.*
I don't understand.	*Je ne comprends pas.*
Do you speak English?	*Parlez-vous anglais?*
Could you please write it down?	*Est-ce que vous pouvez l'écrire?*
How much is it?	*C'est combien?*

GETTING AROUND

What time does the … leave/arrive?	*À quelle heure part/arrive …?*
bus (city)	*l'autobus*
ferry	*le ferry (-boat)*
train	*le train*
Where is (the) …?	*Où est…?*
bus stop	*l'arrêt d'autobus*
train station	*la gare*

I want to go to ...	*Je voudrais aller à ...*
I'd like a ... ticket.	*Je voudrais un billet ...*
one-way	*aller-simple*
return	*aller-retour*
How long does the trip take?	*Combien de temps dure le trajet?*
left-luggage locker	*consigne automatique*
platform	*quai*
timetable	*horaire*
I'm looking for ...	*Je cherche ...*
my hotel	*mon hotel*
the market	*le marché*
supermarket	*supermarché*
a public phone	*une cabine téléphonique*
What time does it open/ close?	*Quelle est l'heure d'ouverture/ de fermeture?*
Where is the toilet?	*Où se trouve les toilettes?*
I'd like to make a telephone call.	*Je voudrais téléphoner.*
How do I get to ...?	*Pour aller à...?*
Is it near/far?	*Est-ce près/loin?*
Go straight. ahead	*Continuez tout droit.*
Turn left/ right.	*Tournez à gauche/ droite.*
behind /in front of	*derrière/ devant*

SIGNS

Entrée/Sortie	Entrance/Exit
Ouvert/Fermé	Open/Closed
Renseignements	Information
Interdit	Prohibited
Toilettes, WC	Toilets
Hommes/	Men/
Femmes	Women

TIME & DATES

What time is it?	*Quelle heure est-il?*
It's (two) o'clock.	*Il est (deux) heures.*
When?	*Quand?*
today/	*aujourd'hui/*
tomorrow/	*demain/*
yesterday	*hier*
morning	*le matin*
afternoon	*l'après-midi*
evening	*le soir*
Monday	*lundi*
Tuesday	*mardi*
Wednesday	*mercredi*
Thursday	*jeudi*
Friday	*vendredi*
Saturday	*samedi*
Sunday	*dimanche*

Numbers

1	*un*
2	*deux*
3	*trois*
4	*quatre*
5	*cinq*
6	*six*
7	*sept*
8	*huit*
9	*neuf*
10	*dix*
15	*quinze*
20	*vingt*
100	*cent*
1000	*mille*

Emergencies

Help!	*Au secours!*
Call a doctor!	*Appelez un médecin!*
Call the police!	*Appelez la police!*
Leave me alone!	*Fichez-moi la paix!*
I'm lost. (m/f)	*Je me suis Ègaré/ée.*

Index

See also separate indexes for Eating (p125), Sleeping (p126), Shopping (p126) and Sights with map references (p127).

EATING

SLEEPING

SHOPPING

Sights Index

FEATURES

Mon Vieil Ami	*Eating*
Moulin Rouge	*Entertainment*
Les Deux Magots	*Drinking*
Notre Dame	*Highlights*
La Samaritaine	*Shopping*
Hôtel de Ville	*Sights/Activities*
Hôtel Jeanne d'Arc	*Sleeping*
Musée Claude Monet	*Out & About*

AREAS

	Building
	Land
	Mall
	Other Area
	Park/Cemetery
	Sports

HYDROGRAPHY

	River, Creek
	Water

BOUNDARIES

	Ancient Wall

ROUTES

	Tollway
	Freeway
	Primary Road
	Secondary Road
	Tertiary Road
	Lane
	Mall/Steps
	Tunnel
	Walking Path
	Walking Trail/Track
	Pedestrian Overpass
	Walking Tour

TRANSPORT

	Airport, Airfield
	General Transport
	Metro
	Rail
	Taxi Rank

SYMBOLS

	Bank, ATM
	Castle, Fortress
	Christian
	Embassy, Consulate
	Hospital, Clinic
	Information
	Internet Access
	Islamic
	Jewish
	Monument
	Museum
	Parking Area
	Point of Interest
	Police Station
	Post Office
	Ruin
	Swimming Pool
	Winery, Vineyard
	Zoo, Bird Sanctuary